Little Stories / Big Ideas

By
W. Hamp Watson, Jr.

CWP
CAMBRIDGE WAY PUBLISHING
Macon, Georgia

THE SALES PRICE: $14.00

Proceeds from all sales will benefit The League of the Good Samaritan of Magnolia Manor, The Homes for the Aging of the South Georgia Conference of the United Methodist Church. If purchased at a United Methodist Church or an institution of the Conference, there will be no additional charge. Add $2.00 for shipping and handling if ordered from W. Hamp Watson, Jr., Cambridge Way Publishing, 149 Cambridge Way, Macon, Ga. 31220-8736. E'mail whwatson2@cox.net, 478-475-1763 All checks should be made out to Magnolia Manor.

Cover design by Lillian Davis

Scripture references are footnoted, but reference no particular Bible version.

SAN: 255-8041
ISBN 0-9746976-2-1

Little Stories / Big Ideas[1]

is

for our grandchildren:

John Hampton Bagwell
Emily Day Bagwell
Hampton Matthews Watson
Jordan Bentley Watson
Sarah Sherman

ALSO BY W. HAMP WATSON, JR.

Frederick Wilson Still Speaks – Big Words for Our Time[2]

More Big Words for Our Time[3]

ACKNOWLEDGEMENTS

Thanks to:

- The Reverends John M. Bagwell and C. G. Haugabook, Jr. for their help.
- Dr. Robert Beckum, Magnolia Manor Vice President for Church Relations.
- Contributors of the stories whose names are indexed within.
- Contributors who gave the funds for the cost of printing so that proceeds could be given to Magnolia Manor's "League of the Good Samaritan."
- Lillian Davis of Macon, Georgia for designing the Front and Back Covers and giving other invaluable assistance.
- My wife, Day, who read all of the stories and then told me exactly how the ones she remembered really happened.
- Katherine Johnson and Victoria Logue, daughters of Dr. J. Frederick Wilson, for permission to use his stories. Special thanks to Katherine for checking the entire manuscript for typographical and diction errors.

W. Hamp Watson, Jr.

---

[1] Benefiting the League of the Good Samaritan at Magnolia Manor
[2] Benefiting the SGC United Methodist Homes for Children and Youth
[3] Benefiting Wesley Glen, SGC Homes for Adults with   Disabilities

Foreword

Some things are just good for everyone involved. Those good things offer people win, win, win situations. This newest book from Hamp Watson represents a win for many wonderful people.

Every reader will be wonderfully blessed and inspired by delightfully heartwarming stories that will make one remember, smile, cry, or sometimes laugh out loud to the glory of God. Every person whose unique story is told will continue to enrich our world in his or her own inimitable way, and the Christian ministry of Magnolia Manor's League of the Good Samaritan, which will receive the proceeds from every book, will be enabled to provide care for God's older children who need financial assistance to live out their final years in dignity. Wow, now that really is win, win, win! I believe that the very heart of God rejoices at the possibility.

We can be grateful to Reverend Watson for LITTLE STORIES / BIG IDEAS. This book is a winner in every way. Join the Lord God in enjoying it!

Bishop B. Michael Watson
South Georgia Area
The United Methodist Church

W. Hamp Watson, Jr.

Contents:

W. Hamp Watson, Jr.

Introduction

Shortly after I selected the title, *Little Stories / Big Ideas,* my friend, Creede Hinshaw, wrote a column for our Georgia Newspapers about the trip he made to bury his father. I had already been convinced that stories had the powerful potential to communicate truth, when I realized how much our Lord depended on parables for this purpose.

But I'm printing Creede's column in its entirety because he says so beautifully and poignantly what I would like to say to you and any other reader before they begin this volume. Here's Creede:

Gathered with family and friends, I stood before my mother and father's tombstone in the country cemetery at Boxley, IN, last Saturday to bury my father. A mile or two from the 40-acre farm where Dad was raised, we laid to rest the last member of Boxley High School's Class of '28.

The preacher read the Bible and prayed and stories of my father's formative years flooded my soul:

About the time my grandfather, who migrated from North Carolina, defeated the strongest man in those parts – a one-armed farmhand – in a wrestling match...about how my father trapped muskrats in the creek behind the cemetery...about a devilish boyhood prank pulled on a friend at the Boxley Methodist Episcopal Church...about my father's wintry ride to town in a horse drawn buggy sitting near a hot rock placed there to keep the children warm.

What remains except our stories?

Ask ten people what the preacher said in church last week. Chances are they'll remember a story. Maybe about Jesus. Maybe about the preacher's pet collie.

W. Hamp Watson, Jr.

Theology is important. But theology gets slippery. No matter how logical and sequential we try to be, no matter how much we strive for order and intelligence, it's our stories that remain.

We sometimes think our "best" writing is the carefully reasoned treatise, passionately written about life's deepest issues.

Yet most columnists soon discover that when we write about our son's broken leg, our mother's third marriage, even (especially!) our pet's trip to the veterinarian, these columns strike the deepest response. People relate to stories.

This column is not intended to be anti-intellectual. Society needs deep thinkers. We must have and share ideas, causes and great themes. We need equations and theorems and manifestoes.

But when one gets to the cemetery, it is the stories one remembers.

With the last notes of taps fading over the Indiana cornfields, final hugs and condolences received, my wife, son and I returned to the car. Leaving the Boxley crossroads I turned west, hoping to find the site where Dad's farmhouse – long since razed - once stood.

Dad had taken my brother and me there when we were children. Knocking on the door of a stranger's home, he told the owners he wanted his sons to see where he first lived. I wanted to connect with Dad on that road. Searching in vain, I spotted nothing to recall Dad's old home place. No particular fencepost or rise in the ground elicited a cry of recognition. It was a good lesson. Everything will eventually disappear. Everything. The sands of time finally will efface even the marble tombstone.

The grass withers and the flower fades, observes Isaiah.

Soon, back in my hometown, I was spinning childhood stories to wife and son. They'd heard these stories before, and I knew it. Maybe they'll pass them on. But eventually nobody will remember them. Nevertheless, today it felt good to re-tell them, and to have listeners.

So said Creede Hinshaw, June 22, 2005.

W. Hamp Watson, Jr.

Let me tell you where most of the stories in this book came from.

Gems from Georgia Giants includes stories from Bishops, fellow ministers, and laity in churches across Georgia This makes up the largest section in the book.

Nuggets from Near and Far has stories contributed by those from out-of-state. Some were prominent leaders in the church. Stories that defied classification were also placed here.

In both *Gems* and *Nuggets*, there are many stories that came as the result of my having been teamed as Song-leader in Preaching Missions and Revivals with some of these out-standing preachers. In those days, as a young preacher, I kept my pen and pad close at hand for fear that I might miss something that might fit in next Sunday's sermon.

Memories from the Manor features a few contributions of stories from Staff and residents of our network of Homes for the Aging in the South Georgia Conference of the United Methodist Church. These homes, scattered throughout South Georgia, are all called "Magnolia Manor." The "League of the Good Samaritan" is a fund enabling Magnolia Manor to keep its promise that no resident will ever have to leave Magnolia Manor because of limited resources. Since the printing costs for this book have been borne by friends of Magnolia Manor, all sales will benefit the "League of the Good Samaritan."

Pearls from Our Pastorates recounts those indelible moments and experiences that came while serving as the pastor's family at Griffin First (Junior Pastor and Minister of Music), Kramer, Liberty Hill, Pitts, Rochelle, Seville, Bethesda, Goshen, Marlow, Rincon, Union, Colquitt, Harmony, Eastman, Grace-Savannah, Bainbridge First, Park Avenue-Valdosta, Wesley Monumental-Savannah, Laurel Branch, and Glenwood Hills United Methodist Churches over a ministry spanning fifty-five years.

Chestnuts from the Family Tree contains stories from the family of Dr. and Mrs. F. H. Wilson of Griffin, Georgia, the parents of my wife, Day. We called her mother "Ma" and her father "Doc." My parental family, Wade H. and Pearl Matthews Watson of Baxley, Georgia, was also a source in this section.

W. Hamp Watson, Jr.

I have not placed all stories that involved a particular name or contributor in any sequence, so one will have to use the index at the end of each section to find a particular story connected to a person. Because of my technology limitations, the index is only accurate within a page or two. On occasion, when I remembered the Scripture that was connected with a *little story* when I first used it in the context of a sermon or devotional, I have placed a footnote. This might be helpful to persons who must give devotionals or to any ministers or lay speakers who might want to explore the *big idea*.

I have made a diligent effort, in my own stories and in those I have edited, to remove as much moralizing as I could. A really good story doesn't need shoring up with such props. You readers have enough sense to bring to the *Little Stories* the really *Big Ideas*. But don't get too upset with yourself if you are not able to find the "big idea." I will confess that at the outset, I put in some of these stories purely for their entertainment value.

Nearly all the stories are authentic, true occurrences. It will be apparent because of context or signals given in a very few of them, that elements of that particular story are not literally true. As Fred Craddock said once at a story-telling session at Brasstown Valley Resort, "The stories that I shall tell tonight are from my memory, and they are either true… or not."

Enjoy! And if perchance you should learn a lesson for life, chalk that up as a bonus.

W. Hamp Watson, Jr.

Macon, Georgia
August, 2005

Gems from Georgia Giants

Bishop C. W. Hancock, whom we know as "Handy" said, "When I was the pastor at Mulberry Street Church, Macon, Mrs. Orville Park was a member of the church. She was a most interesting person. At the time she was in her late nineties. Yet, she was very mentally alert. When I visited her in her home on Orange Street, I found that she was most conversant about current events. She listened to the news. She read the newspaper regularly. She kept up with everything.

Mrs. Park was in and out of the hospital. On a visit to see her during one of those times, she remarked to me: 'Brother Hancock, I do hope that I do not die in one of these hospital gowns.'

I asked her why she had that thought. Her reply was, 'I'd hate to spend eternity backing around in heaven.' Great sense of humor for a woman nearing 100 years of age."

One of our women in ministry, B. J. Funk who currently serves as Associate Pastor at Central United Methodist Church in Fitzgerald, said, "It was my first year of preaching. Sitting in the congregation was a very well dressed older woman. She could easily have stepped out of the church and onto the fashion page of a magazine. Her perfectly groomed hair encircled an attractive face. But, of course, I was concerned about her soul. I knew my sermon was solid in Scripture, with plenty of illustrations that brought home the Scripture's message.

At the close of the service, I made my way to the back of the church to shake hands with the worshipers. What I longed to hear was, 'Pastor, you made me think today,' or 'I want to know more about that verse in Scripture.' I would really have 'scored' if someone wanted to arrange a meeting to discuss his or her relationship with Christ. Of course, none of the above happened.

Then, *she* walked up. As I extended my hand, I wondered what the well-dressed woman might say. Had the Holy Spirit touched her heart?

W. Hamp Watson, Jr.

She welcomed my extended hand, facing me with a slight smile. Maybe she would be the one person who let me know she heard from God! I waited eagerly.

'B.J.,' she said, 'you need to wear a little more lipstick and a little darker rouge.' And with that, my well-dressed lady walked to her car.

So much for saving souls."

Abimael Rodriguez is affectionately known as Pastor Abi to his United Methodist Hispanic congregation, *Iglesia De La Vision*. This "Church of the Vision" now flourishes on the site that formerly housed Aldersgate United Methodist Church in Macon. Abi is in the forefront of the efforts of our New and Revitalized Congregational Development to utilize wonderful facilities bought with the love and sacrifice of faithful Christians who have found their efforts to continue as a church are no longer viable. Aging of congregations and changing demographics can bring an end to the life cycle of a church, but it can be reborn in a new direction with a new constituency.

Abi shared this story with me. He said, "A young man came to my church a while back. A family in my church had invited him to their house because he had no place to stay. It is very normal in the Hispanic community to receive somebody into your house even if you do not know them. This is especially true in the USA. It's part of the warm hospitality practiced among those who are often the poorest people.

But this time was different. It did not take a long time for them to realize that this man was extremely dangerous. The only thing he talked about was different ways of how he was able to kill people. That Saturday night, the situation got very scary to the point that they hid all the knives and silverware in the house. Nobody was able to sleep that night.

That's why, on Sunday morning, they called me and told me that it was very urgent for me to take this guy out of their house. Of course I went and brought him to my house, but it didn't take me long to find out what a mess I was getting into.

W. Hamp Watson, Jr.

That same Sunday, I was trying to explain to this young man that I had to be at church a little early because I had to serve communion. His eyes and face lit up. You have heard the expression, 'Evil Eye?' You would have had to be there to feel what I was feeling as I looked at that face.

At this moment he says, 'I am going to serve communion with you!' This was in a very serious tone, not making a joke at all.

I thought, 'I can't let this unqualified man help me serve communion to my people.' But to be honest with you, I had rather ask God for forgiveness for allowing him to do it than to find out what he would do to me if I didn't. Believe me, it wasn't pleasant to serve communion with this man.

Somehow I got through it; and, you know, after that service, he was more open to me. I had the chance to talk to him and share God's plan for salvation with him. He wanted to go to Atlanta. This was a relief to my family and me. I bought him a ticket and sent him to Atlanta.

I learned that the 'plan for salvation' didn't take immediately because I heard that he was arrested shortly after arriving in Atlanta. But would you believe that two months later he sent me a letter from jail, thanking me for presenting the plan of salvation? He said, 'Pastor Abi, I am serving God here in this jail.'

I don't know what will finally happen in his life, but I always remember that our work in Christ is not in vain."

Attorney Frank C. Jones, long-time member of Vineville United Methodist Church in Macon, recalls:

"Before I moved to Atlanta in 1977, it was my privilege to serve as Chancellor of the South Georgia Annual Conference. Warren Plowden, who succeeded me in that position, worked closely with me. It was necessary in the late 60's and early 70's that we file a number of lawsuits in behalf of the Conference to protect the rights of the ministry and members of the United Methodist Church with respect to local church property in accordance with the *Book of Discipline*. These were situations where the members of local churches had voted to withdraw from the denomination and also "to take their property with them."

W. Hamp Watson, Jr.

For many years, the *Discipline* has provided that even in the absence of the required trust clause, local church property is held in trust for the ministry and members of the United Methodist Church if any one of three things can be shown: (a) the conveyance of the property to a local church of the United Methodist Church or to its Board of Trustees; (b) the action of a local church in holding itself out publicly in the community as being a part of the United Methodist Church; or (c) the acceptance by the local church of pastors appointed to it by the bishop or the Conference.

One of these cases was tried before a Superior Court judge in a South Georgia county. I called for cross-examination a fine old gentleman who had been a member of the local church in question for more than half a century. Beginning with the current date, we went backward in time and he identified every single pastor who had been assigned to that local church during the preceding fifty years or so. In winding up the examination, I recall that I asked him a question such as the following:

'In conclusion, is it correct to say that according to your own personal knowledge, your local church has accepted the pastors assigned to it by the bishop and the conference for at least the past fifty years?'

He thought for a moment and then responded, 'Mr. Jones, we took what we got.'"

When Johnny Deas was pastor of the Leary Circuit, he reported having to drive back to the parsonage at Leary from the Church at Damascus. He said, "I noticed as I left Damascus that the gas gauge showed empty. As I drove toward home, I remembered that the speedometer and the odometer were both broken on that old car. When I got back to the parsonage, I thought about that situation.

Before I left Damascus, where no gas stations were open, the gas gauge told me that I couldn't go anywhere. As I was traveling, the speedometer told me that I wasn't going anywhere. When I arrived at the parsonage, the odometer told me that I hadn't been anywhere. But the greater reality was that I was at home."[1]

Handy Hancock also gave me this one. "When I was the pastor at Dawson Street Church, Thomasville, we had a terrible wind and rain storm to come through the city one night. We had an elderly couple, Mr. and Mrs. R. L. Dameron, in the church membership. They both were quite frail and their illnesses kept them from attending the church services.

The morning following the storm, Mr. Dameron phoned me and said, 'Brother Hancock, the storm that came through last night knocked out our electric meter box. An electrician has been here this morning and tells us that it will require twenty-five dollars to replace it.' (You know that this was some time ago.)

He continued, 'We don't have the twenty-five dollars with which to replace it.'

I said, 'Mr. Dameron, call the electrician and have him replace it and I'll have the money in your hands this evening.'

That afternoon, I carried the money to their home. Before I left, I shared a prayer with them. When I finished the prayer, Mr. Dameron spoke to his wife. 'Honey,' he said, 'get me the box.' She knew what he meant. She opened a drawer and took out a small box and placed it in his hands. With trembling fingers, he opened it. There was money in it. I could tell at once that it was more money than I had brought them to pay the electrician. He spoke and said that he wanted me to take this money to the church for them.

I protested, saying, 'Mr. Dameron, I want you to keep this money and use it for your great needs. I know you must have heavy doctor bills and medicine bills to pay. We're getting along fine at the church. Use this money to help with your expensive needs.'

I saw a frown come across his forehead. His words were, 'Brother Hancock, you don't understand. That's an accumulation of our tithe. That's God's money. There is no way we could use any of it for our needs. That's God's money.'

---

[1] I John 3:19-20

W. Hamp Watson, Jr.

Somehow I made it back to my car through tears that I couldn't hold back."

In January of 1959 I heard Dr. Albert Trulock who was then serving as Pastor of Wesley Monumental in Savannah tell this story. Horace Freeman, the father of surgeon Dr. Tom Freeman of Savannah, grew up in a rural area in Reconstruction Georgia. His was a poor, but proud, family following the Civil War. One of the embarrassments of his childhood was when the Methodist Steward came around for the Quarterage for their little country church. In those days, they didn't have an annual budget and pledge campaigns to underwrite the budget in advance. Administrative Board members called "Stewards" would each take a list. Before each Quarterly Conference they'd ride up to each farmstead on a horse or in a buggy, pulled by a mule, and collect the "Quarterage," that is, the church payments or pledges. Out of this, the pastor would get his salary for three months, and the District Superintendent, or Presiding Elder as he was called in those days, would get his salary and the Conference Apportionments.

Horace was standing there when the Steward approached his mother. He said, "Mrs. Freeman, do you have anything you can give towards the Quarterage?"

Embarrassed, she looked down into her worn apron and said, "Josh, I'm sorry. There's not a dime on this place. Here's a dozen eggs to give the preacher, but we don't even have enough eggs to share any with the Presiding Elder."

Horace was just coming into his early teens. He ran back behind the barn with tears streaming down his face. He knelt down there and the prayer came tumbling out with the tears. He said, "O God, I'll be the Quarterage. So help me God, I'll be your man!"

When my friend, Bill Dupree, was pastor of the Winona Park Methodist Church in Waycross, there was a faithful couple, Hugh and Roselyn Farrior, in the church. They had four young boys. Roselyn's first husband was killed in an automobile accident, leaving her with two boys. Hugh's first wife had died, leaving him with one son. They met, married, and God blessed their home with a fourth son. She told Bill how she was dating another man before she met Hugh. Frequently she told her two small boys, who wanted a Daddy so badly, to pray and God would send them the Daddy they needed. She was feeling them out one day and asked them how they'd like to have the man she was dating as their Daddy.

Oldest one said, "Let's wait and see who Jesus sends." Needless to say, she didn't marry him. She waited and married Hugh.

Stephen Webb, Pastor of First United Methodist Church, Bainbridge, Georgia, told this recently on the front of his bulletin.

"A face like yours," she said. It's my annual inspection; about as routine as a lube job and tire rotation. A trip to the dermatologist, oh boy! The doctor looks me over real good— checks my back, my finely chiseled chest, arms and legs, the tops of my feet, and scalp. Then her eyes lock on my forehead, and the area around my eyes. She gives a long, heavy stare, and then lets out a sad, thoughtful sigh. I hold my breath. She has found something, I am sure. I immediately convince myself it's skin cancer; she's going to have to remove my face to get it all. I'm thinking I'm a goner when she says, "We can do something about all this."

"All of this? All of what something?" I ask. "What?"

"Botox," she says. "All these deep furrows, these crow's feet, the frown lines. Botox can achieve remarkable results on a face like yours."

That's nice, isn't it? A face like mine is what Botox was made for.

Apparently lots of people pay good money for this type of treatment. Doctors shoot this form of botulism in your face and it attaches to the nerve endings, preventing those areas from wrinkling up. Basically it paralyzes the nerves so they don't work.

W. Hamp Watson, Jr.

The result—parts of my face wouldn't move—no facial expression in those areas.

If only we could erase the evidence of the past, or cover up the emotional aches of our present life; dull the senses, paralyze the nerves, feel nothing but numbness. According to my dermatologist, I'd look a lot better if I did that – at least for three months. That's about as long as Botox lasts. Then the wrinkles and frown lines come back, and your true identity is revealed.

Someone said that the lines on our face are a map to our soul. I think I'll just leave my face as it is. You can't really cover up the past; the lines are there and they are a part of my journey and my journey is blessed.

When Creede Hinshaw was pastor at Metter, Georgia, he put this on his bulletin front. "Did you see that article in the paper about 'The Rusty Jesus' up in Fostoria, Ohio? Outside of town sat a rusty silo on which the image of Jesus appeared. A number of people could plainly see Him. When a local radio station publicized the story, thousands of so-called pilgrims drove past the unpainted shrine. The owner, who had been planning to repaint the silo, quickly changed his mind. Somebody with a flair for making an easy profit sold coffee mugs that bragged, 'I saw Jesus in Fostoria', or something to that effect.

The local ministers wisely (and uncharacteristically) chose not to comment. I don't know how they held their mouths. The police chief glibly said, 'Since this has happened, all hell has broken loose!' (This guy could have come straight out of the Gospel of John, where innocent remarks often have more than one meaning.) The editor of the local paper admitted, 'Yes, the image looks like Jesus, but it looks a little like Buckwheat, too.'

If it weren't all so sad, it would be hilarious. Two thousand years after the resurrection, people are still starved for Him. But how misguided! Thousands of curiosity seekers drove to stare at a rusty Buckwheat-Jesus when they could meet Him at the Lord's table. Jesus is not some freak in a sideshow to be gawked at and dismissed.

W. Hamp Watson, Jr.

Dr. Mack Anthony, Pastor of First United Methodist Church in Valdosta, urged his members to leave to go help start Park Avenue. John McGowan remembers voting as a member of the Official Board to buy this piece of property out on the edge of town back during Leonard Cochran's tenure. He told me that his mother, a member of First Church, said, "If Brother Mack gets up there one more time asking people to leave our church, I'm going to kill him."

Truth is, it was painful for Mack. George Zorn, the founding Pastor of Park Avenue United Methodist Church, wrote me that the response was so great on the "sign up" day that Mack returned to his pulpit the next Sunday and said, "Some of you members need to stay at home." So their motivation must have been to spread the gospel and make disciples, if they were willing to go through such painful separation.

George Zorn, the Founding Pastor of Park Avenue United Methodist Church in Valdosta, knew that 1953 wasn't an easy time to begin a new church. The economy reeled from the drought of the summer of 1954 when all the farmers around were hauling water for their stock. But George told me something that explained why this little beginning church could go so far out on a limb that it could make Ned Steele, who followed George, inherit what was then "the biggest debt in the South Georgia Conference."

He told me that the pledge service in the Carson McLane Funeral Home was crucial. He said that in that crowd, where secret, private pledges were to be made on which the future of launching the church hinged, there was a couple—Earl and Libby Winderweedle. After the pledge service Libby and Earl drove quietly home. Hardly a word was spoken. Earl said, "Inside the door Libby seized my shoulders, as frequently she was wont to do. Looking me squarely in the eye, she solemnly said, 'You increased our pledge, didn't you?'

I took her in my arms and said, 'Yes, I couldn't do anything else!'"

W. Hamp Watson, Jr.

The late Ellis Miller, of the South Georgia Conference, grew up down around Iron City, Georgia in a Free Will Baptist Community. He tells about going one time with his grandfather to a Free Will Baptist Association meeting when they were going to have dinner at the church. He said his grandmother got ready for it for two or three days and when the big day came, she didn't carry the food to the church in two or three little trays. They had an old trunk and they put the food in the trunk to carry it to the church. He said he had to help carry it to put it in the back of the truck, and before he left it there, he opened it just to take one last anticipatory look.

He said there were wonders to behold—three kinds of meat, six vegetables, cornbread, (not just little old pan muffins, but real old cornpone).

Then the desserts came, climaxed by a huge bowlful of custard pie, not these store-bought imitation custards in a box, but the real, mouth-watering, old-fashioned custard. He said it took him a while to get his head out of the trunk and his mind out of a trance.

But then they went on to the church where he saw one of the most memorable pictures of his life. His grandfather was ninety-two years old, weighed about one hundred and twenty pounds with snow white hair, but he was still in good health largely because his grandmother just spoiled him to death and waited on his every desire. Because of his great age his grandfather took his place in the corner where the elders of the church sat. It was sort of a ceremony escorting the old saint to his place while he exchanged greetings and warm hugs and handshakes all through the church.

After a few songs, a very young preacher got up to preach. He didn't have much meat in his message, but he flailed away mightily with his arms. When he had been going like that for a little while the back door of the church opened and another really old man was brought in. He'd been sick and out of the church meetings for a while. On a cane he made his way down to the elders' corner and when he saw Ellis' grandfather, his face lit up. Ellis' granddad got up to meet him and the two old men embraced. They just stood there and patted each other on the shoulder while the preacher stumbled on through his message.

W. Hamp Watson, Jr.

They got settled momentarily, but no sooner were they seated than another old man from a church across the county came in. They both got up to embrace him and there were three white heads in a close circle and the quiet patting of each other on the shoulders.

The preacher flailed on and the sermon failed—but the church didn't that day. The church was alive that day in that quiet, touching meeting of brothers.

Later all the trunks were opened and they broke bread together and it was a sacrament of sharing for everyone.[2]

Bishop B. Michael Watson tells this experience from his childhood:

"John tells us, *If anyone does sin, we have an advocate with the Father, Jesus Christ the righteous.*[3] We are told that we have a defender with our Heavenly Father if we sin. What could be better news than that? Every one of us has sinned, and we know it.

When I was a little boy and had done something wrong, I remember having to go before my parents for punishment. Now, I confess that I was forever getting into things. Nothing seemed to escape my attention. I had to find out about everything. I had to try everything.

This type of behavior often led me into trouble, and much of my childhood was spent answering to my dear parents. But, what I remember most about all of those times in my childhood when I was called upon to pay the price for my misadventures was my sister. Judy is nine years older than I am, and she just couldn't stand to see me get punished. Many times when Mother or Daddy would start to punish me, Judy would pitch a fit! She would cry, plead, and beg on my behalf. Sometimes she offered to accept punishment herself rather than see her little brother get what he rightly deserved.

I had an advocate, someone to stand by my side, not because I was right, but because I was loved. I have no way of knowing how many times I was spared because of my sister's loving defense, but

---

[2] I Corinthians 11:23-26
[3] I John 2:1

W. Hamp Watson, Jr.

I can say that I was very sorry to see her go away to college and leave me to struggle through on my own!

My sister cared -- she still does -- and she was able to do more than I could have ever done to plead my case. Because of her, I began to understand how the loving advocate God has given us in Jesus Christ, the righteous, pleads for us not because we deserve it, but rather because we are loved! That is Good News to me!"

I remember George Wright, our former Conference Lay Leader from Tifton, telling about the guy who went into a crossroads country store and found a woebegone storeowner hanging over the counter looking like he'd just lost his last friend. Behind him there was just shelf after shelf full of Morton's Salt. That's all he had on his shelves. The stranger said, "Friend, you must sell a lot of Morton's salt."

He said, "No, I don't sell much Morton's salt. But that fellow that sold me—he sells a lot of Morton's salt!"

My friend Don Kea put this incident on the front of his bulletin for Worldwide Communion Sunday. He said, "On Sunday, July 29, we were in Paris. Our group's first stop that morning was at the Notre Dame Cathedral. As we stepped inside the nave, I felt as if my breath had been taken away. The place was packed with worshippers from all over the world! There were:
- Young people in jeans carrying backpacks,
- Tourists like us, with cameras,
- Africans, North Americans, Japanese,
- Rich poor, and all else in between,
- Native French people from the neighborhood.

I picked up a bulletin for the service and noticed that it was in six different languages. Then the choir began to sing and the priest spoke—all in French. I couldn't understand a word that was being said, but there was no doubt about what was happening. The body and blood of Christ was to be shared, the Word of the Gospel was

W. Hamp Watson, Jr.

to be proclaimed! In spite of all the differences that could be found that day in that crowd, I felt a universal spirit and purpose![4]

Jimmy Chester told me that he had a layman who said to him, "Jimmy, my wife literally saved my life." He said that for years they had had the habit of nightly devotionals. This couple got down on their knees and held hands across a chair before they got into bed. A recession came and he lost everything he had. With the recession came his deep depression and he planned to take his life the next day. He had the gun and the spot picked out. But that night he said, "I heard my wife call my name before God in prayer."

He said, "She literally saved my life."

If you've ever been a sibling, or if you've been a parent of siblings that didn't get along very well, maybe Frederick Wilson's story will give you hope. I heard Frederick talk about his older brother, John.

He said, "John was three years older than I, so that means that he was three years older than I all along the way. And that was just enough to make it bad—just enough to make it bad. He was constantly picking on me and I was constantly aggravating him— mainly by telling him, every time he did anything, 'I'm going to tell Mother on you!' If I said that once in my life, I said it ten thousand times. And I don't know why he didn't kill me... really. That was the only thing I knew to say or do. I had no muscles. I couldn't do anything about it. You can look at me now and tell what I must have been like at eight or nine or ten. And he would do something to me and I would say, 'I'm going to tell mother on you—tell mother on you!'

And he wouldn't say anything, just hit me again—and here we'd go. Oh, I hated him. I really hated him. And he just tolerated me. I wouldn't accuse him of hating me, but he just tolerated me— that's all. At night we slept together in the bed. I never saw a single bed, it seems to me, until late in my life. We all had double beds.

---

[4] I Colrinthians 11:23-26

W. Hamp Watson, Jr.

We had to sleep together—no choice. One night he pushed me to the foot of that bed—literally pushed me! And I deserved to be pushed. I had taunted him about the things I was going to tell Mother that he had done that day. And he got so angry with me he just pushed me to the foot of that bed. There must have been six quilts on that bed, because there was no heat in the room, you know, and that's all we had, just quilts. And I thought, 'Oh, God, I'm going to suffocate under here! He's not going to let me up! He's not going to let me out!' Finally I bit part of a foot that was coming at me. I was fighting back a little bit and he let me out.

Daddy had about five or six sisters who lived in our town. One day he'd invited them all over for lunch and we were all at the table. John and I were there at the table, and somewhere along in the conversation, Aunt Lizzie, the oldest one of his sisters, said, 'Brother John, what do you think about your boys?'

We were both sitting there. It wasn't two days before that John and I had gotten into one of these things and Daddy had sent us out to the peach tree to get a switch. Now if you think that's a mission that you can relish—to be sent for your own switch—it's just about the worst thing that you can think of. And we both came back and he took us to the bathroom, where he usually took us for things like that. He handed John his switch back and he handed me mine. Then he said, 'Switch each other! I'm tired of doing it myself.'

And he just stood there to watch us. John would hit me; then I would hit John. That had happened not two days before. And Aunt Lizzie dares to ask, 'Brother John, what do you think of your boys?'

John and I wanted to go under the table. 'What is Daddy going to say?'

And what Daddy said was, 'Sister, they're not bad boys. As a matter of fact, they're good boys.'

Lord, have mercy. What was Daddy trying to say? He was trying to say to John and me, 'I believe you're good boys! I believe you have the potential of being good boys. And one day, you will be good boys. I believe that.'

In spite of all the evidence to the contrary, he believed in us. And for the sixty-nine years of his life, he did believe in us. It was a

W. Hamp Watson, Jr.

part of that faith he had in us of what we could be—the young men, and the men that we've become. And he did love us; and more than loving us, he believed in us." [5]

John went off to college—came down here to Valdosta. We had a fine black woman that came to help us at the house in those days and she set the table for lunch. And she set John's plate. She didn't know he was already gone. So Daddy came home from the store and we sat down to lunch and there was John's plate. Mother started crying, and Daddy got choked—couldn't eat. And I thought to myself, 'This is the most foolish thing I have seen in my whole life!' Because mother, when Daddy asked her why she was crying, didn't say anything. She just pointed to John's plate over there.

Oh, about an hour later upstairs in our room, I got to thinking about it, and dadgummit! I started crying, too. I realized I did love John. I really loved him, and just started crying. Not because I missed him, I was glad he was gone, but I just realized that I loved him.

I heard the late Dr. Cecil Myers of the North Georgia Conference say that he hated to ride in airplanes though his work often called upon him to do it. He was afraid and would get nauseated at times. He claimed it made him sick just to have to lick an airmail postage stamp. But he said, "I found a way to make myself feel better while I'm on a flight. Before I leave the airport, I buy the maximum amount of insurance on myself, and I think the whole time I'm up of how much I'm worth."[6]

B ishop Pendergrass went in to buy something in a store and presented his credit card. Thinking the clerk might want some more positive identification, he said, "I'm Edward Pendergrass."

---

[5] John 17:14-20
[6] Matthew 6:26

W. Hamp Watson, Jr.

The clerk hardly looked up at him as she said, "I don't need your name, I've got your number."

Now, I'm grateful for the convenience of a credit card, but this becomes serious when it becomes the way we see our fellow human beings—numbers to be exploited and used it they are respectable and agreeable to us or good credit risks, and numbers to be avoided if they are "bad numbers."

Bishop Roy Nichols told about going to a camp meeting as a child when some of the people would "get through" to God down at the altar. They'd get up singing,

> I looked at my hands and my hands looked new.
> I looked at my feet and they did, too."

He said, "This isn't just the "old time" religion. I'm talking about the "all time" religion."

My friend, Creede Hinshaw, reports that an outfit called Tornado Research is trying to discover a correlation between church attendance and tornado or lightning victims: Do tornadoes seek out non churchgoers? They asked these questions of a pastor after lightning killed one of his members: Male or female? How old? Affiliated with the church? Did the person go to church: once a year, occasionally, regularly, or very active in church work?

Just think of the implications if they discover that tornadoes and lightning seek out the backsliders! Church pews would become full again. Offering plates would overflow. Evangelizing Bibb County and the world would be a snap. We could scare heaven into people. Maybe insurance rates for regular attendees could be reduced, too. What a revival would take place!

I wish it was that easy, but Tornado Research won't have much success with its surveys. The Biblical testimony from Job to Jesus has been that tornadoes are not choosy.[7]

---

[7] Luke 13:4

W. Hamp Watson, Jr.

The old Preacher-Philosopher Charlie Ledbetter, of our Conference, fought catarrh when he spoke. When Guy Hutcherson introduced him to me, while I was a student at Candler, the first thing he said to me was, "Son, harumph! harumph! Can you say 'Bob,' without putting your lips together?"

I tried mightily, but I couldn't and said, "No, Brother Ledbetter."

He solemnly put his forefinger between his lips and said, "Bob!"

It was from Brother Charlie that I first learned about the law of the necessary minimum that we apply in much of our lives. Somebody asked Brother Ledbetter, when he was serving at Rhine, Georgia, why he hadn't married again after his wife died. He said, "Next woman I marry will have to be as rich as Mrs. Rockefeller, as pious as Susannah Wesley and as pretty as Mae West."

But most men are content with less. Does she love me? Can she cook and run a family? And, these days, "Can she earn half or more of the living?" Can she keep her mouth shut long enough for me to tell her all of my problems? Then I'll marry her! I know enough. This is the law of the necessary minimum.

I don't want to be flippant about a serious subject, but what about the things that happen that make no sense—the tragic things in life? Why is there calamity, why insanity, why cancer, why polio, why birth defects, why tsunamis? I don't know. I only know the character of our great God can be utterly trusted. God is love and cannot be false to God's nature, and I count on that. This is the necessary minimum for living. *The secret things belong unto the Lord our God, but the things which are revealed belong unto us and to our children forever.* Is that enough? Is that enough for you? I hope so.[8]

I thought of Carlton Anderson when I talked to a young guy at a block party on the street where I live. He was discouraged because the huge tobacco company he worked for was transferring him and his family to Louisville, Kentucky. It made me think about the tobacco farmer in Carlton's church. This was way back before most of us were aware of the massive destructive

---

[8] Deuteronomy 29:29

W. Hamp Watson, Jr.

death toll of the industry. The farmer was sick, so Carlton had a prayer for him before he left. The burden of the prayer was that the man would soon get well so he could go back to work. When he finished the man said, "Preacher, it's all right to pray for me to get well, but don't pray for me to go back to work. I hate my work."[9]

A son of Southwest Georgia, who couldn't respect his father, was called to his father's hospital room. In a moment of rare confession, his father said, "Son, when I came to these parts, I worked hard and pushed a lot of people around. I wanted to build up a fortune in this property to leave to you. On the next farmstead there was another man who wasted his time going off to church and conferences. He'd sometimes let the grass eat him up, sitting up with a sick neighbor. I got a piece of his land illegally, but he wouldn't take it to court. I thought he was a fool, for he never had anything and sure wouldn't get it that way. But you know, he brought up all his children in the church and saw that they all got a college education. That man is the richest man I know. I've been wrong."   (That reference, "the richest man I know," is to C.S. Pryor of Leslie, Ga., once Conference Lay Leader of the South Georgia Conference of The United Methodist Church.)

My friend, Tegler Greer, told of going into a home on his charge. He noticed a map of the world on the wall of the den. He especially noted one spot on the map that was dirty, as though it had been pointed to many times. He said to his host, "Why is this one spot on the map here so soiled?"

The father in the home said, "Oh, we have a son stationed there in Turkey."

Have you ever wondered why God is so interested in our world?[10]

---

[9] I Corinthians 7:17
[10] John 3:16

W. Hamp Watson, Jr.

Claude Fullerton told me about an UN-winsome Christian girl. Her boy friend screwed up the courage to ask her father for her hand in marriage, like we used to do in the dark ages. Her daddy said, "You can have her, but I want to be honest and warn you. She's hard to live with."

The suitor said, "But she's a Christian, isn't she?"

Her father said, "Yes, but there are a lot of people God can live with that nobody else can."

When Bill Hurdle was in high school in Montezuma, Georgia, he went by and told his English teacher that he was going into the ministry, and she said to him, "You must have lost your mind!" She could remember how timid and shy Bill was when he first hit her classes. When she would ask, "Do you have your essay ready?" he was so terrified that he couldn't say, "Yes." He would just nod his head.

She'd say, "Will you read it to us?" It was the same story. He'd just nod his head the other way. He was so shy he could hardly answer the roll.

How did one so paralyzed by fear get to be the pastor of Mulberry Street United Methodist Church in Macon, a District Superintendent and finally Director of the Georgia Methodist Commission on Higher Education? Somewhere he must have learned that when he saw the wind, and was afraid, and was beginning to sink, he could cry, "Lord, save me!" and a hand would immediately reach out to him.[11]

Hurdle also told about a man in his home church at Montezuma on whom the church could always depend. If they were short of Conference Askings or Apportionments, he would cheerfully make them up with a large year-end gift. He was constantly lending a hand to people in need, would spend hours on odd jobs at the church and would even try to patch up arguments among the brothers and sisters. Bill asked him one day why he did so much and where he got the energy to do it.

---

[11] Matthew 14:22-23

W. Hamp Watson, Jr.

He said, "Bill, one night when I was a little boy I was critically ill. The doctor came to my house and said, 'Unless his fever breaks, I don't believe he's going to make it.'

Later in the night, I heard my Daddy praying at the side of my bed. He prayed, 'O God, if he can just get over this and live, I promise that I'll do all in my power to see that he'll always be your man.'"

He looked at Bill and said, "I guess you could explain all the things I try to do by saying that I never have caught up with that promise."

Bill Willis told me about an alcoholic friend of his in California who didn't believe in God. It angered him to suggest to him that as the second step in the AA Program he was to pray to a higher power, for "only a power greater than ourselves can restore us to sanity." He refused this step. AA told him, "Well, you are certainly allowed to be in our program regardless, but it works best if you pray to some kind of higher power, something bigger than you."

So the guy picked out a big bus to pray to. He said, "That's bigger than me." He talked to that bus, and prayed to that bus, following the steps of AA. As he got progressively better, he said to himself one day, "You're pretty stupid to be praying to a bus." So he started praying to God like everybody else.

Tom Johnson, Jr. was four years old and helping his Daddy pick up paper and trash on a work day in front of their church at Bloomingdale. Little Tom was following along behind his daddy, helping and hindering, gathering and scattering.

Earlier in the clean-up day, some member of the church had given little Tom a pack of chewing gum. Becoming generous, he had eaten a piece, but had also given a piece to his daddy. Big Tom didn't want it for himself, but rather than deny the child the chance to make a gift, he took it, thanked him, and put it in his pocket. Later, Little Tom discovers that he has lost the other three pieces out of his pocket. He begins bawling. They look for them. No

W. Hamp Watson, Jr.

gum. Tom, Jr. is inconsolable. Then, Big Tom remembers the piece of gum Little Tom had given to him. He takes it out of his pocket, says, "Here, Son, here's the piece you gave to me."

The crying ceases, as though you had shut off a water faucet. And if you talk to Little Tom today, he'll tell you what he learned that day. Only that, which we have given to our Father in this life, will be finally ours. We will lose all the rest.[12]

D r. Glenn Burton, down at Tifton, who was a great agricultural scientist, said that somebody needs to teach the church to spell service—S E R V I C E. He said that most of the members have been spelling it...S E R V E US...serve us. He said that most people tend to judge a local church or preacher on the basis of how well that church meets their needs, rather than thinking, "How can I best serve Christ and my Church?"[13]

D uring a Sunday-School class he taught at Vineville after his retirement, Frederick Wilson made a confession about when he was at Albany First Methodist Church in the sixties during all the racial problems in Albany. He said something like this: "I thought what shall I do? Shall I stand before my congregation and say, 'We should open the doors and let all these black people come in. Oh, I know we are a white congregation. But are there some whose pride makes them forget that blacks are humans, too, and children of God?' Should I just explode with this kind of opposition to the general feeling toward black people? Shall I turn in my resignation because the people don't want the black people to come in? What to do? What to do? I feel for these people and I want something better for them. So is this the way to do it? So, not secretly at all, but not broadcasting it or publicizing it either, I worked behind the scenes and would go to talk to the black leaders. Not just to solace my conscience but to try to do something without causing an explosion.

---

[12] Luke 12:20
[13] Mark 10:35-45

W. Hamp Watson, Jr.

And in one of my moments of agonizing prayer, 'God, what to do? What to do?' I didn't hear a voice, you know that, but I felt something so strongly inside. God said to me, 'The race problem is mine. Not yours alone. The race problem is mine and I will take care of that. I put you in this vineyard.' Jesus loved that word. 'I put you in this vineyard; this is the church where you are assigned. And what you are to do is to love this people and hold them together.'

Well, maybe that was plea-bargaining. Maybe that was just trying to ease myself. But this is the feeling I had to come to. What good would it do if I walk out and leave this church; rip it to disruption that would maybe require years to recover from, while I wind up as the pastor of a church in New Jersey? Or, on the other hand, shall I try to do what I can quietly to foster acceptance and reconciliation without that kind of an explosion? It's bothered me a lot, even yet, when I think about it. Why aren't you out there with others who made the open break and sacrificed their careers as a witness?" So questioned Frederick Wilson. Have you been there?[14]

When Frederick Wilson was pastor down at Jeffersonville in Twiggs County, an elderly woman was very ill and he went to see her often. Almost every time she would say, "Oh, if my boy would just come home. Oh, if my boy would just come home to see me, before I die."

The son was in Atlanta, which isn't so far from Twiggs County. So Frederick called him and told him his mother was very sick and he thought he needed to come home to see her. He couldn't judge how long she might live, but she wanted to see him.

The son replied, "I'll try to get there."

He did not. But when she died, he came. As Frederick stood there talking to him after the service, he was thinking, "I just wish you had made this visit before your mother died. I think it would have been more important for you to have come then, than to be here now."

---

[14] John 19:38-42

W. Hamp Watson, Jr.

About that time the son said, "Didn't we put her away nicely?"[15]

Somewhere in South Carolina early in the twentieth century an English divine, a clergy-person, came over to preach on an exchange and go quail hunting. A Mr. Smith had a plantation with several coveys and entertained the Englishman at his home and carried him quail hunting. When the birds got up, the excited Reverend ran in the direction of the birds to shoot and came under fire from his host or from someone in the host's hunting party. They rushed him to the nearest doctor, but he died from loss of blood.

Devastated, Mr. Smith contacted the man's family, did what he could to compensate them, but then tried to put the horrible incident behind him. It was a rule in the house that it would never be a topic of conversation.

Some children were born to the Smiths and when his son came home from college one Christmas, he approached his father and said, "Dad, I know you have wanted me to carry on this farm. But I have to tell you that I have given my heart to the Lord and I feel compelled to enter the Methodist ministry."

Mr. Smith broke down in tears and for the first time in his life told the man who was to become Bishop John Owen Smith where he got his name. The English clergyman's name was John Owen. Mr. Smith said, "Ever since you were born, I have been praying that somehow you might be called to take the place of that good man."

John Owen Smith became Bishop of the Atlanta Area of the United Methodist Church just in time to guide us through the perilous sixties, as integration came to church and school. He always said, "This is our time! This is our time!"

Charlie Shepard Pryor, former Lay-leader of the South Georgia Conference, over at Leslie, Georgia, told Thomas H. Johnson, Sr. a story that reaches back into the roots of his family. He had a single great-aunt who kept a hope chest only half-

---

[15] John 19:38-42

W. Hamp Watson, Jr.

heartedly because time was passing and no man had asked for her hand in marriage. But a hired hand came on the place in Sumter County and worked for a while for her father. He didn't openly court her, just eyed her across the water pail or the dinner table where she served them. Before he left to go back to North Carolina, where he had come from, he asked her to marry him. He gave her a little ring.

She'd never known him before, never knew his family, and when he left to go back to North Carolina he told her it would be some time—maybe a year or two before he came back to get her and marry her. He said he had to work out the debt on his place for a homestead, and then he'd come. So in the months that followed, his aunt filled her hope chest and sang and hummed joyously around the house. They tried to tell her that he wasn't coming back, but she'd say, "He said he would." The months stretched into a year, then two years and she didn't hear from her fiancée. The family sadly tried to counsel with her and discourage her from having her hopes so high. Girl friends scoffed, and the father patiently, tenderly explained that he might have changed his mind or married someone else. Dozens of voices would say, "He's not coming back." But always her answer was the same as she looked at her little ring, "He said he would."

One day, two and a half years later, an unfamiliar carriage drove up the long lane that led to the house. From the front porch they all wondered who it might be. Finally, the former hired hand stepped out of the carriage and claimed the hand of the aunt who wore the little ring. They were married; and she put her hope chest in the back, got in the carriage, and went off with him to North Carolina where they raised a fine family. "He said he would." And he did.[16]

In the laity address at Annual Conference, Sylvia Powell told about seeing a Church of God in a little town with a sign out front, with letters where the last letter was missing in the title of the church. Instead of Church of God, it said, Church of GO. But you know, that's right. If a church is going to be a Church of God,

---

[16] II Corinthians 1:18-22

W. Hamp Watson, Jr.

it's going to have to be a Church of GO! It'll have to be a church where the pastors follow up on every visitor who comes to the church. Churches, where the lay people invite and follow up, nearly always grow.

I remember Dr. Zach Henderson, the President of Georgia Southern when it was called Georgia Teachers College, telling how his daughter grew up, went off to college, and asserted her independence. One day when he saw her with a cigarette, she said, "Daddy, I'm grown now. I'm free. I can smoke. I'm free to smoke."

He said to her, "Honey, ask yourself whether if you smoke it's because you are free or because you are slave to the group approval of five other girls in your dorm who smoke?" For that matter who is free that's addicted to a substance? Until somehow we reach out and find the power that helps us to throw it off, we are slaves and we know it.[17]

When Jim Laney, former President of Emory University and ambassador to Korea, first went into the army at eighteen, he was in basic training in a large barracks. There were double deck bunks on both sides of an aisle. The first night they undressed in their own little sheepish way, trying to get into their own beds without being too exposed. There must have been eighty to a hundred fellows in that barracks. And just before lights went out, the fellow next to Laney on the bottom bunk knelt down to say his prayers. At first there was a shocked silence. They'd been boisterous. And here was this figure, kneeling down beside the bunk. This was a most unlikely sight in the army, in the barracks, in basic training. The fellow's name was Bracey. It was the only name that Laney remembered after all the years.

After a moment of shocked silence, the place erupted in derision. "What's the matter, Bracey, you homesick? Ya' miss ya' mama? What kind of stuff? What are you saying down there, Bracey?" You know how raucous and contemptuous young men

---

[17] John 8:34

W. Hamp Watson, Jr.

can be with each other, especially when you show a kind of residual habit from childhood. Everybody wants to swagger and be big. Here was Bracey saying his prayers. Laney was up on top of his bunk, ashamed that he wasn't down on the floor with Bracey, but he said, "I wouldn't have gotten down on that floor for a million dollars."

Laney was curious the next night to see whether Bracey was going to do it again. Just about the time lights went out, Bracey got down again. Well there were a few cat-calls. But it had lost its charm. So people kind of left Bracey alone. The third night nobody said anything. Bracey got down. He did it every night during basic training. Of course he was a pretty good sized fellow, strapping guy. At the end of basic training, his company elected Bracey as the most highly respected cadet. Well, even if that hadn't happened, you know, we can get too sophisticated trying to be more cosmopolitan than the world. But what is appreciated in the long run and what makes an imprint on the world is steadfastness of character.[18]

Dean Jim Laney, of our Theology School at Emory, told how some years ago there was a young woman whose parents were missionaries in India. She came to Emory as a graduate student having already received the Master of Divinity. She became ill with leukemia. And after a while, (this was a galloping leukemia) she went into Emory Hospital, became very, very ill, and was obviously going to die. They wired her parents in India, and her father came back. They were Australian missionaries to India.

The Dean visited this young woman, in her fevered state, after her father had come. This was a fairly large single-bed hospital room. Her father, who was a missionary, was sitting over by the window reading. And here was Anna, lying in her bed at the other end of this narrow room. You could feel the enormous gap. The father, who had come such a distance, and yet still seemed so far away. After going in and out a couple of times in frustration, not

---

[18] Romans 5:1-5

W. Hamp Watson, Jr.

knowing what to do, the Dean shared his frustration with the nurse on the floor.

The nurse's eyes lighted up. (Now this is competence, practical wisdom, and imagination.)

She said, "I think maybe I can do something about that."

A few minutes later a cleaning person went into the room with a mop and a bucket and said, "Sir, you'll have to move down to this end of the room."

And once the chair was down there, the nurse came in and she said, "Oh, you know, I think that's just where you ought to sit."

The dean, who was outside listening, walked in a few minutes later and here was the father, sitting by his daughter's bedside. The dean said a few words and left. A few hours later he came back into the room. The father was holding his daughter's hand and singing the songs of her childhood. It was just an absolutely indelible moment. The father was a minister of the old protestant ethic, severe and remote, unable to express his feelings. And the daughter, dying, needed so much to feel her father's presence. That nurse, with knowledge and practical wisdom, addressed the feelings of frustration and incompetence on the part of the theology dean. That nurse had probably put his hand into hers.

When the dean visited Anna the next day, it happened that she was alone. And she smiled in her wan way, and she said, "You know my father and I have never been real close since early childhood. And his singing to me was a sign of deep reconciliation." She was prepared to die. That was a great moment, made great by knowledge, practical wisdom. It's not just the intention. The dean had the intention. It was the trained nurse who had the knowledge, the competence, the practical wisdom to bring it about.[19]

When Kell Hinson moved in as pastor at Springfield, Georgia, he and Mildred had just one child, a little redheaded boy named James Lee. But the Sunday School Superintendent mistakenly thought that there was a little girl in the family, too. So when he saw James Lee come into Sunday School

---

[19] Romans 5:1-5

W. Hamp Watson, Jr.

that first Sunday, just making conversation with the little boy, he said, "James Lee, where's your little sister?"

James Lee shot back at him, quick as a flash, "Don't you know if I had a little sister, she'd be at Sunday School?" You see, there are some things you expect of the Hinson Family.

I heard Jack Key tell about a leading citizen of Albany, Ga. whom he met at the YMCA one day. A racial question came up and the man's face turned red and he pounded his fist in his hand and said, "I've made up my mind about that. I'll never change." Ooh...that's dangerous. A man like that may wind up with a tombstone that reads like one I heard about:

"Here lies Harry Herman. Died at 45 - Buried at 85."

Former President of Emory University, Jim Laney, told us that there was a marvelous quotation in the Atlanta paper back when the NCNB Bank was acquiring C&S, which later became Nations Bank, America's Bank and now Bank of America. They asked the Chairman of the Board, "Why do you want to buy C&S?"

He said, "Because you got to feed the tiger."

You know what that means? "You got to feed the tiger." In that atmosphere all comparisons are money related.

A fellow banker was asked, "Why does that man want to keep on making so much money? He can't spend it." He said, "Well, that's his way of keeping score." Those were his exact words.[20]

Dr. Jim Laney also told us, at Minister's Week in April of 1999, about a student at Emory named Sharon Carr who was dying of brain cancer. He said, "She will probably not live to see graduation." So he and the dean of the college drove over to Augusta, where she lived with her parents, to see her and to present her with a real Emory Degree. This was not simply as a

---

[20] Luke 12:20

W. Hamp Watson, Jr.

matter of pity, but because she had written some of the most sensitive and faith-laden poems that any of them had ever read. Floyd Watkins, Candler Professor of English, said, "In 39 years of teaching at Emory, I've never seen anything like it." Such poems, such religious poems, such marvelous poems! And through her poetry, she was able to talk to God and to talk to others in her own witness. In one of them she said:

It was a small voice, insistent, exonerating, sensitive, and unflinching. It pulsed at the base of my neck, in that cavity between spine and brainstem. "Sharon," the little voice said, "the dying time has begun."

I know you are here, Immanuel, for every once in a while the red tide recedes and the light of your smile shines blue. I know you are in agony, Haschim, and out of love your bruised wounds lie bare. You came to me in my loneliness in the cross of your son.[21]

My body is trembling. Rottenness seethes in my bones and the flock is cut off from the fold. The scars across my head are stinging as thy wrath against the rivers, and I'm weary of being a rag doll amidst beauty, stitched together because she fell apart.

I'm waiting for the day of trouble, the day when my puppet parts no longer have to be prodded and I can dance with you. The fig tree hath no blossom, Lord. And the final fruit has fallen from the vine. Only the rag doll has reason to rejoice, for there will be dancing upon the high places.

One fall I went to help Sammy Clark in a Revival Meeting. This brilliant graduate of Union Seminary in New York, married to Betty Claire, who graduated in music from Wesleyan, was serving Inner City Methodist Church in Savannah. They chose to go work with displaced people in a government housing project

---

[21] Luke 2:34-35

W. Hamp Watson, Jr.

area in Savannah. Sammy didn't live in a nice parsonage away from there and just visit in this community. He and Betty Claire lived in a two-room apartment slum flat that housed a study hall and Sunday school space. It was a storefront church, and they lived in the community like their people.

Because we were going to have supper after church we were visiting right at suppertime out in Riverside Gardens on the edge of Sammy's parish area. Riverside Gardens was anything but a garden. In Savannah it was known as the end of the line for people on the downward drift. A hundred and fifty families were living out there in three-room broken down hulls of buildings rented at exorbitant rates to them by absentee land-lords who made no improvements and sent around strong-arm men to collect the rent. Sammy had started Thursday night services in a rented unit of the Gardens itself, and he had a summer worker living in it and a few families had started coming. We went to see one of these families.

When we were let in by two of the children, we heard the mother and father railing at each other in the kitchen. The gist of the argument was that there were five children, a household of seven to support, and no work for three months. The father was a skilled shipyard worker, but the ships he worked on had quit docking in Savannah. When the children and the mother saw Sammy, they flocked around him crying, "Oh, Sammy, Sammy!" They poured out their hurt and shame. When they were quieted a bit, Sammy went into the kitchen to talk to the father who was guilt-ridden with his responsibility and his inability to meet it. He talked and cried and Sammy listened.

This isn't a total success story. We didn't find the man a job. But while we were there, the crying stopped. The guilt and bitterness cleared from the air. It was only forty-five minutes until church time, but they all came together that night as a family and every night that week. The guy hadn't been in church in years. They began to talk to each other without panic or recrimination and had a new determination to face their difficult situation. I don't know whether they made it or what's happened to them since, but I know this. Sammy sat where they sat; he came where they were and the Word became flesh and dwelt among us.[22]

---

[22] John 1:14

W. Hamp Watson, Jr.

I ran into The Reverend T. O. Lambert at Conference one year. At that time he was over eighty and working as a Retired Associate Pastor at St Luke in Columbus. I said, "How are you doing, Brother Lambert?"

He said, "My voice hasn't cracked, and it doesn't quaver. My memory hasn't failed and my steps don't totter. I haven't lost my interest in people, and I haven't lost my faith in God."[23]

I remember our dear friend, Dr. Comer Woodward, who, in his late eighties, helped marry Day and me. I called him "Uncle Comer" and his wife "Aunt Mary" because though childless, they took college students like my Dad into their home to help them through Emory. When I was at Emory, he was retired, and I'd run into him in the dining hall where a raft of students had gathered round to hear his stories. He'd start one, but he'd warn you as he started, "Now if I should tend to grow garrulous or long-winded and keep you longer than I should, please warn me and let me know. I know that we older ones have a tendency to do this. Or you just get up and leave when you have to go to class and maybe I'll eventually get the message." He consciously fought acquiring those annoying habits that make us want to avoid many old people and he was deeply and widely loved until he died near ninety.[24]

I loved the Rev. Charlie Jackson, who died close to ninety years of age. Back in 1946 he wrote up an incident for the Wesleyan Christian Advocate that occurred in his first appointment. He said, "That one incident set the tone for all the rest of my ministry."

He said, "Both were old. She was crippled, alternating between a crutch, a wheelchair and the bed. Each month, they received $17 from the County's poor fund. (This was pre-social security for

---

[23] Deuteronomy 34:7
[24] Deuteronomy 34:7

W. Hamp Watson, Jr.

farm folk.) It was my first visit to their farm home in Terrell County, Georgia, during 1932.

If I had known their financial situation, I wouldn't have accepted the invitation to stay for the noon meal. Near the open fireplace were two glasses of buttermilk and a hoecake. They were embarrassed and I was too. Without thinking, I told a white lie— that I had already eaten. My conscience said to me, 'Son, you'll do penance for that lie. If you have fifty invitations today while you are out visiting, you'll refuse. This day you will fast.' I gave the blessing. While they ate, we talked about hoecakes and fireplaces, farming and our little church. When I stood to leave, she wheeled to a drawer, taking out two envelopes, already prepared. She said, 'In case we can't make it to church, here's our offering. And here's something for that Christmas Mission Special you wrote everybody about.'

Holding the envelopes in my hand, I couldn't accept them. However good the cause, they needed it worse. I said, 'You can't afford this; you keep it. There's somebody else who will give it.'

She laughed and said, 'Brother Jackson, you don't understand. This is our tithe. It isn't ours to take back. Giving this is like saying our prayers or singing in church. It's one of the ways we worship God.'

Charlie said, "I went down the road singing. Sure enough at the next farmhouse I stopped they were having late lunch. As was the custom, I was invited to join them. I said, 'No thanks, I have already eaten.' I felt as Jesus did when his disciples returned with food after his encounter with the woman at the well, and he said, 'I have food to eat you don't know about.'[25]

Leigh Ann Raynor, the Pastor of First United Methodist Church in Thomasville, went back to the church she had just left - Christ United Methodist Church in Warner Robins - to officiate at the funeral of a young man. Before she left that church, she had promised Will Bush that she would come back and preach his funeral. He was only twenty-two years of age.. When he was seventeen, Will was diagnosed with a very rare form of sarcoma; in

---

[25] John 4:32

W. Hamp Watson, Jr.

fact, this cancer was so rare, the doctors at Emory had never seen a case in a person Will's age - only in old people.

Will was a remarkable young man. He had been the President of his youth group, lettered in track and field in High School, was near the top of his class, had been chosen as a Star student. But Leigh Ann told us not just how he lived, but how he died.

Most of us pastors have been with people, who, at the point of their deaths, saw things that the rest of us couldn't see—things that were really there for them, but that were hidden from everyone else. Some will say that as people die, they are getting no oxygen to their brains, and they are having hallucinations. But it's strange, isn't it, that most who say they saw something as they died, say they saw spiritual things? "There are angels in the room;" "I see God;" "I see Jesus."

Will was talking, up until about 15 minutes before he died, and then lost that ability. Suddenly, after 15 minutes of silence, he opened his eyes, sat up, pointed out into the room and said, "Little girl! Little girl!" His mother looked around the room, and assured him that there was no one there. Again he pointed and said, "Little girl!" then slumped over and died.

Later that morning, when his mother Terry got online on the computer to send e'mails to people to tell them that her son had died, before she could send her e'mails she received an e'mail from a woman named Michelle. Michelle is a participant on the sarcoma newsgroup on which Terry and Will also participated. Michelle's daughter, Katie, died several years ago, also of a rare sarcoma. She was only 8 years old. Will, of course, never knew her. Michelle's email to Terry said that she was praying for a peaceful passing for Will, and that she had prayed that God would send her little girl, Katie, to take Will to heaven. So, go figure this!

Leigh Ann Raynor, Pastor at First United Methodist Church Thomasville, Georgia recalls how Joyce Elliott, who is a member of Christ United Methodist in Warner Robins, told her a wonderful story that happened in her family. Leigh Ann tells it this way:

W. Hamp Watson, Jr.

"Joyce's late husband, John, was career Air Force, so they had lived all around the country and in other countries, including Turkey. When they returned home from their tour of duty in Turkey, one of their four children, Julie, was still a small child. There were things that small children in this country had seen that Julie never had. One of those things was a K-Mart. Julie had never been in a large store like that, and she certainly didn't have any experience with a voice coming through a speaker system, announcing a Blue Light Special.

That's exactly what happened on her first visit to K-Mart. At the time of the Blue-Light Special announcement, however, Joyce had stopped in one of the aisles to chat with a friend she hadn't seen in awhile. All the while she talked to her friend, two things were happening. One was that the Blue-Light special was being announced over the PA, and the other was that Julie was pulling on the hem of her dress, trying desperately to get her attention. 'Mama, Mama!'

Finally, Joyce stopped talking to her friend and said, a bit exasperated, 'What is it, Julie?'

'Mama, hush! God is trying to tell you something.'

Do you think that God still speaks? I do, and I think God speaks in a variety of ways, including audibly."[26]

We have dear friends, Elick and Margaret Bullington, who are retired and they don't play tennis for exercise, but they walk a lot. And while they're walking, they pick up trash along the highway. I said to Elick, "What do people say to y'all?

He said, "Well, some people think that we're demented. Some think that we've been given community service by a judge. Some think we're prisoners, working on the side of the road."

"Well, then, why do you do it?"

And he said, "We can't stand for things to be so trashy."

Out there—picking up other people's garbage. It's just a little thing. But don't knock it, it's needed. What if everybody did it? What a wonderful world!

---

[26] I Samuel 3:1-10

W. Hamp Watson, Jr.

When he was in college at Emory University, Sammy Clark said, "My roommate's name was Fleetwood Maddox. There were two slots for names on the dormitory door, but I had not bothered to put my own name up. I was studying, but Fleetwood was in Chemistry lab. Two seminary students came in the open door and said that they were concerned about the fact that most Emory freshmen did not have a personal experience with Jesus. Then they launched in with their 'evangelism?'

They asked if they could pray with me. They had already asked me if I were saved, and when I told them that I was a Christian, they told me that being a church member was not enough, that I needed a personal relationship with Christ. Then they prayed, 'Lord help Fleetwood see the light. Lord please send your Spirit into Fleetwood.' And on and on.

When they finished the prayer, they wished me well and left the room. When Fleetwood came in, I told him he'd been prayed for. I couldn't get over the fact that they never even asked me my name."[27]

For thirty-five years, C. G. (Ceegie) Haugabook was a pastor and preacher in the South Georgia Conference before his retirement to Plains, Georgia, where he and his wife, Allene, restored her family home. His call to the ministry centered on the death of his first wife, Joyce Parks. They married on June 18, 1950. She died on July 20, 1951. The night before her death, they had gone to the Montezuma Country Club where she began to cough. Since she was pregnant, they went home. He fell asleep, but, due to her coughing, he woke up about two a.m. His mother and father came and Dr. Tom Adams was called. Joyce was carried to the hospital where she died about 6:00 p.m. It was very dramatic and captured the attention of the town.

Her death had a religious impact on Ceegie's life. He became intensely interested in the Bible and church. His grandmother gave him Peter Marshall's book, *Mr. Jones Meet the Master*. His reading was so intense that he could quote from it almost verbatim. He was not interested in anything but religion. His mother and father

---

[27] II Timothy 4:5

W. Hamp Watson, Jr.

became concerned about his emotional stability. His minister, Mac Johnson, assured them that there was nothing happening that should alarm them. But when his grandmother intimated that he might be going overboard, a crisis was created in his life. He began to stay awake night after night into the wee hours. At a late night hour, he said to God, "You have got to tell me what to do! I am going to let my Bible fall open and I am going to put my finger down." His finger went down on[28], *"And when they bring you to trial and deliver you up, do not be anxious beforehand what you are to say; but say whatever is given you in that hour, for it is not you who speak, but the Holy Spirit."* What leaped from the page were the words: *"it is not you who speak, but the Holy Spirit."* He interpreted it as a call to preach. By September, he was a student in Candler School of Theology at Emory University.

Now Ceegie would no more recommend today that anyone just go to the Bible and flip through it to find God's meaning for one's life than I would. The Bible became for him a book of diverse theologies. Doubt became a prominent aspect of his faith. He found faith to be a process in which he learned to doubt his doubts. But here is his experience, and how else do you explain it? Could the Holy Spirit come to interpret the mind of Christ to us in times of crisis?[29] Could it be as Ceegie put it once, "I learned to use the worst to glorify the highest?"

This same Ceegie told me about a compliment he once received that he could have lived without. He said, "In those first five churches I had on the Americus Circuit, sermon preparation did not come easy for me. Sometimes I found myself wondering on Saturday night what I going to say on Sunday morning. Maybe this is the reason I had the following experience with three sisters in one of the five churches. When I finished preaching, the three sisters came up to me and said, 'Brother Haugabook, that was the best sermon we ever heard you preach. We wish all those people who say you can't preach could have heard that sermon.'

---

[28] Mark 13:11
[29] John 16:13

W. Hamp Watson, Jr.

I stood there and quietly bled."

Allene Haugabook said, "I was teaching second grade at Furlow School in Americus in the early 1950s. At this time the movie "Cinderella" had just come out. I had to leave the classroom for a brief time and asked the children to be as quiet as a mouse while I was gone. I reminded them that I never knew of a mouse that talked other than Gus in Cinderella.

One very talkative little boy quickly replied, 'Well, Miss Timmerman, I think I'll just be Gus.'

I was sure that he would be. Going by daily experience, I could count on him for that."

During the first summer of the civil rights demonstrations in Savannah, Sammy Clark and his Summer Associate, James Walker, were upstairs in the Inner City Methodist Church going over Vacation Bible School materials. The Savannah Police Station was only a block from the church and a noisy demonstration started. The voices began to float up through the open windows of the storefront church building. Sammy and James walked out on Oglethorpe Street to see what was happening.

They didn't know that a leaderless crowd that had been left rather wild was just then breaking up and running in all directions away from the police station. Before they knew it they were in the midst of a confused, running crowd. James' mother, who lived in the country out from Tifton, had warned him before he came to Savannah not to get involved in any of those demonstrations; and when they realized what was happening, they turned around to go back to the church. They were laughing with each other about what James' mother would think if she could see them now.

About that time, a big demonstrator passed them and heard them laughing. He said, "So you think it's funny, do you?" And with that he began hitting them with the leg of an old table that he used as a club. He hit Sammy over the eye and when he threw his hand up to protect himself, the table leg broke his finger and a

W. Hamp Watson, Jr.

bone in his wrist. James Walker's cheekbone was shattered. They both had to be hospitalized briefly.

Sammy said it was really a funny experience for he was visited in the hospital by both sides. The establishment came to see him because he had been a victim of those terrible demonstrations. Civil rights leaders brought him flowers and asked for an audience with him to show their remorse for what had happened to one of their strongest advocates in Savannah in a demonstration that had gotten out of hand. He said it was rather pleasant. He was being treated like the hero of both sides.

But the interesting thing is what this enabled Sammy to do. When clergy and business and civil rights leaders met in the mayor's office to talk about their grievances and the property damage that had been done, Sammy was there with his bandages and black eyes—living testimony to the fact that something had to be done about these demonstrations where sympathetic, innocent persons could be hurt. Sammy helped lead toward the granting of concessions by the city and the cessation of demonstrations. Long before Atlanta adopted the slogan, the unflappable, forgiving, suffering Sammy helped Savannah become the "City too Busy to Hate." When people have followed the foolishness of the cross, they've found this to be the most powerful force in achieving the purposes of God.[30]

Marcia Cochran, Pastor of First United Methodist Church, Waycross, Georgia recalls, "It was 1978. Allison Morgan and I had just been ordained as the first women elders in the South Georgia Conference. I was serving my second year as Associate Pastor at First United Methodist Church in Americus, Georgia. Jimmy Carter was President, so each Sunday we had lots of visitors who were visiting Plains and Sumter County.

During one particular Sunday worship service, I led the congregation in The Apostles' Creed and the prayers. Gene Cariker preached the sermon. We were both dressed in black robes with green stoles.

---

[30] I Corinthians 1:18-25

W. Hamp Watson, Jr.

After the service, I was standing at one of the front doors greeting people when a couple stopped to shake my hand. Noting that they were visitors, I welcomed them to Americus and the church. The woman with a very northern accent said, 'We enjoyed the service today, and I must say how surprised I was to see you. In the north, we don't have women acolytes!'"[31]

Bishop Richard Looney recalls, "My first Bishop (Roy Short) was a saintly man who had the ability to laugh at himself. He was to speak at a large, downtown church in Chattanooga. As he made his way across the street, he met an elderly woman and helped her across the street, and up the high steps. When they reached the top, she asked who was preaching that morning. The Bishop, in his modesty, said, 'I understand that the Bishop is.'
She quickly said, 'Would you help me back down, please?'"

Looney also said, "When I was a young preacher, several of us had gathered at Granny's Chicken Palace just off the grounds of Lake Junaluska. We were having a great time sharing stories and enjoying each other's company. We were laughing uproariously. Someone heard our waitress say to another waitress, 'Do you see that table over there? They are so drunk they think they are Methodist preachers.'"

Frank Terry recalls this incident from Bishop Richard Looney's tenure in South Georgia:
"During my stint on the Cabinet, while serving as Superintendent of the Dublin District, I drove a smaller Toyota Camry, an economical car, in my travels across the district. We also needed to trade for a family vehicle and I had found, in Columbus, a very good buy in a used, older model Cadillac. It proved to be a good decision, but I think Bishop Looney was a bit uneasy, thinking that the laity might misinterpret this as a materialistic bent of both the District Superintendent and the Bishop.

---

[31] Acts 2:18

W. Hamp Watson, Jr.

Whenever Bishop Looney came to our district, I always offered him the choice of the little Camry or the larger, more comfortable Cadillac as we went forth on our visits to the churches. Without fail he always responded, 'Let's go in the Camry.' So he would fold up his giant frame and squeeze into the smaller car.

Finally, one Friday night, justice was done, or at least I thought so. Bishop Looney called me from just outside Dublin. His automobile had been hit by a deer and damaged. He was able to drive to the repair shop I recommended. He learned that it could be repaired, but not until Monday; and he was due at Epworth By the Sea for a speaking engagement on Saturday. Charlotte and I invited the Looneys to spend the night with us; and the Cadillac was freely offered for transportation to Epworth. On Monday they could return to Dublin and pick up their car for the remaining trip home.

He accepted, and I thought I had finally convinced the bishop that he could be happy and comfortable driving an older luxury car. When they returned on Monday he thanked me for our kindness, but meekly confessed that he had parked the Cadillac behind one of the buildings at Epworth, some distance from where he was staying, lest it be seen as belonging to him."[32]

Bebe Cook, a layperson and storyteller from Vineville United Methodist Church in Macon, Georgia loves to tell about the time she was telling stories to children at the Methodist Home in Macon.

She said, "It was near Thanksgiving and I had placed on the board the letters for T H A N K S G I V I N G in descending order. I then asked the children to think of some things for which they were thankful to place under each letter. We started with T and they listed toilet paper, toys; terriers, and so forth. But immediately, little Dalton said, 'Miss Bebe, Miss Bebe, when you get to G, I've got a good one!'

I said, 'OK, Dalton, when we get to G I'll be sure to call on you.'

---

[32] I Thessalonians 5:22

W. Hamp Watson, Jr.

It's a long way down to G in Thanksgiving, and just about after every letter Dalton would hold up his hand and say, 'Miss Bebe, Miss Bebe, don't forget. When you get to G, I've got a good one.'

I would assure him, 'Dalton, I won't forget. I'll be sure to call on you.' We finally arrived at G and I said, 'All right, Dalton. Tell us what you're thankful for that begins with G.'

Dalton said, 'Gesus!'

Immediately there was an outcry. The other children all exclaimed, 'Miss Bebe, Jesus doesn't begin with a G. That's not the way you spell Jesus!'

I said, 'Well that's the way Dalton and I are spelling it for today.'"

B ebe also told me about a device she uses with adult groups and children to get them to listen, and focus on the stories she is telling. She said, "It's an old doggerel poem I learned as a child. I tell my listeners that there are seven things wrong with this story, and when I get through, I want them to tell me the seven things.

One bright day in the middle of the night,
Two dead boys got up to fight.
Back to back they faced each other,
Drew their swords and shot each other.
A deaf policeman heard the noise
And came and killed the two dead boys!
If you don't think my story is true,
Go ask the blind lady, because she saw it too."

She said, "I find that if I go through that little exercise, when I get to the Bible stories, they are quiet and listen and hear a lot more."

I guess Bebe is in a pretty good line of storytellers here. Didn't Jesus say when he told parables, "Let anyone with ears to hear listen?"[33]

---

[33] Mark 4:23

W. Hamp Watson, Jr.

Our former Bishop Ernest Fitzgerald's wife, Frances, recalls one morning when they'd risen at 4:00 A.M. in Atlanta, to drive down to dedicate a Church in South Georgia, and she said to him, "Tell me again why it was you wanted this job?" But we're glad he accepted it. Before and after he was made Bishop, you'd take a flight on an airplane in the Southeast and find his articles in the airline magazine on the back of the seat in front of you. He'd mesmerize your mind with his stories and change your heart for the better with his warmth and wit.

The late Tom P. Watson, who practiced practically his entire ministry after a leg amputation, would delight congregations with a half-moon grin that lit up his entire face when he'd say, "You know, there are advantages in having only one leg. That's right. There are advantages in having only one leg. You know I never did like to wash my feet."

Tom loved to tell about the time when he was at Pembroke and was host pastor for the United Evangelistic Mission. This was a swap-out with the Florida Conference. South Georgia Preachers were paired with Florida Preachers and they exchanged Pulpits for the week of the Mission. Tom said, "I drew a wonderful old gentleman near the end of his ministry that came to Pembroke as our preacher for the week. We had pulled out all the stops, had gotten the Baptists to call off their Sunday night service to come over and join with us, and we had people practically hanging out the windows.

But the old gentleman was pretty dry, and by Monday night we had about half as many. By Tuesday, we had about a third as many; and by Friday night when it was to close, with a paid quartet that we had come in to sing, and my wife and four daughters, we wound up with about twenty-three people.

But I had to hand it to the old boy. When he came down out of the pulpit on Friday night, he said to me, 'Brother Tom, I believe if you would give me another week, I could empty this place.'"

W. Hamp Watson, Jr.

Growing up in Adel, Georgia, V. L. Daughtery, Jr. had this experience:

Covers Dixie Like the Dew, was the slogan used by one of Atlanta's daily newspapers. As a lad in Adel, Georgia, I was the newsboy for early morning distribution to businesses and homes.

Upon rare occasions late breaking news or broken presses would not allow departure from Atlanta on the film express trucks traveling south on US 41 to the Florida line. The circulation manager would telephone the night policeman in Adel to convey the message that papers would be arriving by train.

On a cold February morning before sunrise, I rode my bike to the Southern depot to await the train. It was too cold to linger outside, so I went into the passenger waiting room. A group huddled around a potbelly stove trying to coax heat from new coals placed against dying embers. There was a farmer and his wife from the county, and a widow with three small children.

Without intending to do so, I became a witness to their story of grief and poverty. The widow's husband, a sharecropper, had died a premature death. She had to vacate their home to make way for a new farm family moving in the next month. A relative, a nephew in Miami, had told the uncle who stood in the circle that he would find housing for his aunt and her children if she would travel to South Florida.

Soon we heard the train announcing its approach by shrill blasts at crossings two miles to the north in Sparks. Then we left our warmth; all went outside and watched the passenger cars stop.

My papers were thrown to the ground from the baggage car. I began folding for delivery around the town square. As I worked, I could not help but see the farmer-brother of the widow unbutton the bib pocket of his overalls. He brought out one of those snap-at-the-top men's pocketbooks that seem to unfold forever. Using his fingers he retrieved something from inside that pouch and placed it in his sister's hand.

The local couple stood there until the train departed going south with the widow and her three children. Not until the engineer warned the crossing in Cecil did the local farmer and his wife turn to leave.

W. Hamp Watson, Jr.

Without intending to do so, my steps, while pushing my bicycle, were behind theirs as they moved toward an old automobile. I heard this woman say to the man, "You know, don't you, that ten dollar bill you gave to your sister is all the money we have in this world."

"Yes", he said softly, as he took her hand in his hand, "But we still have each other."

Disciple is a peer group study of the Bible taking place across the span of a year. Participants must spend thirty minutes in personal daily reading and study and agree to be present each week for over two hours of classroom teaching and discussion. V. L. Daughtery, Jr. tells this story:

As the leader for Disciple Bible Study, I prepared large signs printed with the theme of the individual session to be attached to entrances, bulletin boards, walls, and even chairs.

One Sunday afternoon, I invited my visiting five-year-old grandson to assist me in preparing the classroom. The theme of the week was "SIN". With the aid of masking tape, the word "SIN" was placed everywhere. As we finished, Gil looked at me and asked a question. "Grandfather", he inquired, "What is sin?"

As a proud teacher who had motivated such interest in a lad of five, I provided an answer his developing mind could understand. As I finished, Gil asked me a final question.

"Grandfather", he said emphatically, "If 'SIN' is that bad, and God doesn't like it, why are you advertising it?"

When F. J. Beverly headed our Evangelism and Church Extension Office in the South Georgia Conference of the United Methodist Church, he traveled to Pooler to preach one Sunday morning. The host pastor was Simon Peter Clary. Before F. J. preached, the choir got up to sing. They sang *His Eye is On the Sparrow*. Some choir members were absent that morning, so they had quite a struggle with the first and second stanzas.

As the organist played the interlude preparatory to their starting the last stanza, Brother Simon Peter got up and waddled

W. Hamp Watson, Jr.

up to the pulpit. As he began to speak, his wife who was in the choir immediately behind him, tugged on his coattail and said, "Daddy, we're not through."

In a whisper that could be heard to the back pew, Simon Peter said, "As far as I'm concerned you are. It appears to me that y'all have about picked that bird clean."[34]

When A. Jason Shirah was preaching a Revival at Abbeville for his brother-in-law, Reece Turrentine, I heard him tell this:

"Some years ago I was summoned to preach in a series of services in St. Augustine, Florida. During those days I became acquainted with the church caretaker. He was a retired letter carrier from up east and found his place on the church staff.

The conversation one day drifted to a sizable project in which he was engaged. It was the construction of a boat that he declared would be ocean going. I was amazed at his story.

One morning at breakfast with the minister and his wife, I related the conversation with Henry, the boat builder. I recounted his startling assurance that it would be fit for the seas. My breakfast companions laid their forks on the table and sat back in paroxysms of laughter.

'Henry and that boat!' one of them said. They told me that it was ever so slowly taking shape in his garage at home. The motor was already installed. He would do a little work on it each day, although it was far from finished. After minimum work on it, he would take his seat within reach of the motor, crank it up, and listen to it hum—Mmmm! Sounds good! He would sit there with a far away look in his eyes and dream of places he planned to visit transported in this creation of his ingenious imagination and skill. Then he would cut off the motor and go on to other things. For months he had followed his obsession with few signs of progress.

Every day he would go into the garage, crank up the motor, listen to it hum—Mmmm! Sounds good! Then he'd cut it off and go on to other things. It was like the ship of a church or an

---

[34] Luke 12:6-7

W. Hamp Watson, Jr.

individual spiritual life that envisages great things, the mechanics in place, but idling, and never puts out to sea."

One of the "Characters" in the South Georgia Conference of the United Methodist Church in years past was the Reverend L.D. McConnell. He had come into the ministry later in life, after a shot at professional baseball. At Dooly County Camp Meeting, several of us younger preachers were marveling at how he just kept on preaching with power and conviction when lightning had knocked out the transformers and plunged the Campmeeting into darkness. I said, "Brother Mac, how could you just keep on preaching like that in the darkness, without any manuscript or notes or anything?"

He said, "You can wake me up in the middle of the night, and I've got a sermon!"

Dr. A. Jason Shirah recalls this about him. "Among my happiest of assignments was First Church, Valdosta. One of the conditions that appealed to me for a time there was the presence of a choice friend, L.D. McConnell, in a nearby town. At intervals, Mac would show up in the door of my office unannounced. We were both Methodist preachers and shared some of the same disappointments and triumphs, regardless of the size of our congregations.

When Mac made his appearance, I would invite him to sit, which he seldom did. I would sit back in my desk chair and relax for the pleasure of his performance. Mac would stride from one side of my office to the other, making pronouncements on every conceivable subject with startling finality, pounding his fist on my desk and catching my eye in transit for approval. It was always one of the better happenings of my day.

On one occasion in the midst of one of Mac's most vigorous episodes, he turned his head toward the sofa above which was a portrait of John Wesley. He halted in his tracks like a bird dog pointing a covey of quail.

W. Hamp Watson, Jr.

'Hello, John,' said Mac. 'If you were here, you would give me a good appointment!'

He thought his contemporaries did not appreciate his genius. He had to call on history to vindicate him. The truth of the matter was that Mac made every appointment a good appointment, no matter where he was."

Dr. Edwin M. "Buddy" Cooper, Jr. while pastor at Central United Methodist Church, Fitzgerald, Georgia, heard this story:

"When Dr. A. Jason Shirah was serving Central, the church decided to build a social hall and new Sunday School rooms on the property they had purchased from the Catholic Church, which had stood next door for nearly fifty years.

In the discussions the Board decided that if there was a sponsor for it, a chapel could be included in the plans, but someone would have to give it! They turned this over to Jason to pray about and think about as he considered whom he might approach. The three Dorminy sisters, Eulalee, Frances, and Thelma, came to his mind because they had recently buried their parents who had been pillars of the Church.

On a Sunday afternoon, he requested a meeting with the sisters in the Church parlor. They didn't know why they were invited, but graciously accepted their pastor's invitation. He laid before them the idea of a chapel dedicated to the glory of God and to the memory of their parents. All three began to cry. Jason didn't know what to think. Was this too soon after the parents' death? Had he been callously insensitive to the level of their grief and had he approached them too soon? Was this good news or bad news?

Finally Thelma gathered herself together and said for all three, 'You would allow us to do this?'

It was as though they had thought of it and longed for it, but had only refrained from the gift for fear that their motives might be misunderstood.[35]

The Dorminy Chapel now blesses a new generation and will probably continue to bless generations to come."

---

[35] II Corinthians 8:3, 9:7

W. Hamp Watson, Jr.

Gilbert L. Ramsey recalls, "When I was a boy of seven or eight years, we lived in a house which was near a large building. This building was the lodge of a secret fraternal order. We boys played all around the lodge, but never entered it.

We heard stories that men rode goats in the building and that there was a casket inside. Our childish curiosity got the better of us and we were always checking the door to see if it was locked. One day, late in the afternoon, we found the door unlocked! We pushed the door open and climbed a long flight of stairs. We confronted another door which entered into a large, gloomy room. The scene was scary. We began exploring the room. We did not find a goat or a casket. However, what we did see frightened us to death.

High on one wall was a gigantic eye through which the afternoon light was shining. As you looked at the eye, it appeared the eye was staring at you. No matter where you moved the eye was always watching you.

I do not remember who began running first, my buddy or I. But we surely set an Olympic record as we ran out of that room and down the stairs. We were sure the eye was still following us!

For years this experience shaped my understanding of God. He was the great EYE IN THE SKY. He watched everything that we did. He knew every thought we had. There was no hiding from Him.

Several more years passed before I came to see that that eye, while inescapable, was also all-benevolent ,so that I could come to the place where I could affirm, His Eye is On the Sparrow and I know he cares for me."[36]

Gilbert Ramsey also reminded me of the incident when Bishop W. N. Ainsworth was the Pastor of Mulberry Methodist Church in Macon, Georgia. Through his vision, Mulberry conceived the idea that Cherokee Heights Methodist Church should be started. Pastor Ainsworth engaged a powerful young evangelist, Arthur J. Moore, to come and preach in a Tent Meeting Revival on the site for two weeks. At the conclusion of the meeting, Ainsworth was embarrassed to present the love

---

[36] Luke 12:6-7

offering to Arthur Moore. It was a small depression era pittance, unworthy of his expenditure of love, sweat and tears, if not blood. He said, "Arthur, please allow me to give you something from my salary to supplement this." Arthur Moore refused the money and nothing Ainsworth could do availed to persuade him to take it. As a gentle argument ensued, Arthur J. Moore was unyielding in his refusal to take the money.

Years later when Ainsworth had become a Bishop, Arthur J. Moore received a telegram from him appointing him as Pastor of the prestigious, huge Travis Park Methodist Church out in San Antonio, Texas. Thereafter, Arthur Moore always maintained that he had been more than compensated and even out-maneuvered. He said, "I guess Bishop Ainsworth finally won that argument after all."

Bishop James E. Swanson, Sr., who was elected from the South Georgia Conference of the United Methodist Church to serve the Holston Area, said:

"I guess the story from my life that continues to bless me was from when I was serving my first appointment as the pastor of the Statesboro Circuit. The Circuit consisted of four congregations. The four churches were Charlestown, Springhead and Goloid, all located in Screven County, and one in Statesboro, Brannen Chapel.

Willie Edward Benton was the Charge Lay Leader and the Charge Pastor/Parish Relations Chair. Benton called me one morning, in about my second month of serving the Charge, and invited me to lunch, but he was coming by about 9:00 a.m. to pick me up. Well, sure enough, about nine he showed up and off we went. He said to me, 'Rev. Swanson, I thought it would be good for me to show you around Screven County so you would know how to get around.'

I think I might have mumbled something, 'Sure.'

We began our tour of about a five-mile radius of the three churches and along the way he would point out a house and say, 'Now, Mr. and Mrs. Hunter live there. Dough Daniel lives there. The Williams family... they live back up in there.'

W. Hamp Watson, Jr.

He would add as we passed some homes, 'Now, Rev., they haven't been to church in some time. The man who lives in that house has been sick for a while now and I can't recall the last time someone served him and his wife communion. This guy has a good job, but he never gives to the church. This family stopped coming to the church when we had a split several years ago and now they don't go to any church at all. The lady that lives there is not a member of our church. She is a member of the Baptist, but in times past, she attended our church every third Sunday. I wonder why she doesn't come anymore.'

Now, this went on for about an hour and finally, I asked him, 'Bro. Benton, are you trying to tell me something?'

He stopped the truck and looked at me and said with a curious look in his eye, 'Why, Rev. Swanson you are the pastor. I wouldn't dare try to tell you how to do your job. Now, if you saw something that is stirring in you, then maybe you need to let the Lord tell you what to do.'

And with that he headed back to Statesboro and we went to Kentucky Fried Chicken and had lunch together. But, when he dropped me back off at my home, I got in my car and did some visiting in those two counties. And for his visit that day I am eternally grateful.

I guess there were some gaps in my theological training that I had received in seminary, but Bro. Benton was determined to fill in one of the gaps."

Before he was a Bishop, I heard Frank L. Robertson tell about Florence, a member of St. Luke United Methodist Church in Columbus, Georgia. Florence had a friend in a club, who progressively became an alcoholic. She confided in Florence and Florence told her one day after their sharing session, "You are going to be my Number One Project!"

From then on, Frank said, "Whenever I would see them, they were together—at the grocery store, on the street, or making a call in a home, I'd find them together."

Frank said, "This went on for a year or two until this friend of Florence started coming to her Sunday School Class. After Three years, she was the teacher of Florence's class!" Her Number One Project!

As I remember it, I think Frank was talking about how God often imposes burdens upon us, but it's the healthy Christian who sets out in faith to do something about them.[37]

Thomas A. Whiting finished his active ministry as the Pastor of Peachtree Road United Methodist Church in Atlanta, but his roots were in South Georgia where he had served as District Superintendent and the Pastor of several churches. At a Camp Meeting one morning, I heard him tell a little more about his roots. He told about his Junior Class Teacher in the Camilla Methodist Church. He said, "She took such an interest in every child in her class. In my senior year in college at Emory, I made my decision to preach and I sat down and wrote her to tell her what a far-reaching influence she had had on my life through the three years I spent in her class. I wanted her to be one of the first ones to know.

My mother wrote later to tell me that when she got the letter, she rushed down the street and burst into my mother's house with tears of joy as she exclaimed, 'I never knew I meant so much to those boys!'"

She must have been one who had prepared her heart to seek the law of the Lord, and to do it, and to teach.[38]

The eccentricities of Bishop William R. Cannon are legend, but I did not see them "up close and personal" until I led singing in a Revival he preached for C. E. "Ned" Steele at Porterfield United Methodist Church in Albany, Georgia. His penchant for avoiding colds and even the hint of a sneeze from others was matched by his obsession with avoiding foods that would set off his allergies.

When we arrived on Sunday night, Evelyn Steele had prepared a lovely salad meal for us at the parsonage. Before we helped our

---

[37] Numbers 11:11-17
[38] Ezra 7:10

W. Hamp Watson, Jr.

plates from the sideboard, Bishop Cannon asked, "Is there any seafood in these salads?"

Evelyn assured him, "No, Bishop. There's no seafood in any of the salads."

As the week progressed and we ate in other homes, the Bishop would poke around in the salads or casseroles and ask, "There's not any seafood in this, is there?"

Since Evelyn had amply warned every woman in the church, the hostess would always assure him, "O no, Bishop. There's no seafood in it." This went on in several homes.

Finally, on the last night in a home, the Bishop poked around in the salad and was assured that there was no seafood in it. He then poked around in the beans on the table and said, "There are not any onions in these beans are there?"

Again, the hostess assured him, "O no, Bishop. There are not any onions in the beans."

Bill Cannon said, "Well, that would have been all right, because I can eat onions."

I always had the suspicion that he reveled in his eccentricities and would spend a week consciously planning how he could showcase them and amuse his companions.

Beverly Flowers, Pastor of Asbury United Methodist Church in Savannah, Georgia, relates:
"I was a newly assigned pastor at Joycliff United Methodist Church in June, 1997. Upon arrival, we immediately noticed that the church sign was terrible. It had no function; it had small lettering; no one made any changes to the message. If the small church sign did get changed, none of the people in the cars passing by could read it because it was a short sign hiding behind a tree. We literally did not like that sign but it was too early to say anything. I could not say a word to this new congregation who had never had a female pastor. It was too early to even attempt to form a Committee for the Church Sign. So, we began to pray and talk to God the father about this church sign.

I knew that our God answers prayers, even though I may not know when, and I may not know how, but I trusted that God's delay was not necessarily a denial. So in 1998, sure enough, the Lord sent a major storm to Macon that knocked down the sign and completely destroyed it. The church was able to get the insurance funds to erect the present church sign. It was featured in one of the articles in the Macon Telegraph dealing with local church signs around the city.

Some folk often make fun of those who boast that they were at the Mall, and couldn't find a parking place, and they prayed to the Lord and suddenly one opened up. They believe that these people want us to think that they have a hot-line, direct connection that will keep them from ever suffering any inconvenience. But to me, this was a miracle, and out of this experience, my faith and that of the church was increased, as I have shared this testimony. I learned that there is no issue too small to tell our heavenly Father about. If it's an issue that God is also concerned about, then we do not always have to have a committee meeting to solve issues.

The church can pray and find her answers and true 'Happiness is the Lord', even if it does not turn out the way we might have wanted it."[39]

S everal years ago Don Saliers, our teacher of Worship at the Candler School of Theology, was with a graduate of Candler in Florida named Gary. Gary said, "Today, we're going to see Myrtie."

It was near Christmas, and since Don was visiting at Gary's church, he went with Gary to the one-story old building that housed people in wheelchairs. He said, "We entered the door and there were people along the hallways, some nodding, some staring blankly, some with wonderful, beautiful, little Christmas wreaths on their housecoats."

Down the long hallway, through those smells that only those places have, they went—went to the last room on the right at the end of the hallway. He met Myrtie.

"Hello, Myrtie," Gary said. "We're here from church."

And Myrtie said, "Oh Boy!"

"We have some gifts from the children at church", said Gary.

---

[39] II Corinthians 12:7-10

W. Hamp Watson, Jr.

So they sat down on the bed, and Myrtie said, "Oh Boy!" And one by one with her one good hand and with some help from Gary and Don, she opened up the little Christmas gifts—here a Christmas ball; here, a piece of peppermint.

"These are gifts from the kids to you. They sent them."

And to each she said, "Oh Boy!"

They talked a little bit, really just Don and Gary, for these two words were the last remaining vestiges of a once profuse vocabulary. Then Gary said, "I brought communion."

"Oh Boy!"

Then the small piece of bread, in the hand. "Oh Boy!"

Then the trembling small glass, which always, I think, reflects our heartbeat. "Oh Boy!"

They made a few more comments and then were out the door and down the hallway. Just as Don was getting in the car, Don looked back and there, at the window, in the end of that long wing in that place, she stood. Her one hand was parting the curtain slightly, and he looked, and though he couldn't hear it at that distance, he saw her lips moving, "Oh Boy! Oh Boy! Oh Boy!"

It was the only language of gratitude and praise she had left. [40]

I love Bishop John Owen Smith's story about being lost on the back roads of South Georgia on his way to a meeting. He was trying to get his bearings. He saw on his map that he should be near a town named Ambrose. He stopped at what he thought was a country store, rolled down the window, and asked a man, "Where is the town of Ambrose?"

The man said, "If you'll just get out of your car and put your feet on the ground, you'll be waist deep in Ambrose."

I heard the late Dr. Cecil Myers tell about the fellow that went into a church and the preacher made a good point, so he said, "Amen!"

The preacher made another good point, so he shouted, "Hallelujah! Glory!"

[40] Job 19:25-27b

W. Hamp Watson, Jr.

He was disturbing the other worshippers, so an usher came over and said, "Look, brother, you can't do that in here."

The man said, "But I'm happy."

The usher said, "I don't care if you are, you can't do that in here."

The man said, "But I've got religion."

The usher said, "Well, you didn't get it in here, so shut up!"[41]

One of our women in ministry in the South Georgia Conference of the United Methodist Church is Karen Prevatt. She's extra small in stature but at a Savannah District Ministers' meeting where I heard her give the devotional, I learned that she was a little woman with big ideas. She said,

"I had taken a group of high school seniors to Epworth by the Sea to their last 'Epworth experience' as youth. We had a heartwarming weekend and were in the van two exits away from Richmond Hill UMC when the group began begging to return to Epworth for one last good-bye. We were four hours ahead of schedule for our arrival time, so I eventually agreed to turn around and go back.

As I was exiting I-95 on the way to EBTS, one of the girls began to wail, 'I've lost my retainer! I know I left it at Epworth! I must have thrown it out with my lunch! My parents are going to kill me! They have already replaced the first one I lost, I can't go home without my retainer!' The sobs increased until we drove under the Epworth arch and jumped out of the van to head for the dining hall.

After explaining our dilemma, we were informed that the dining hall trashcans had already been emptied into the dumpster. We said, 'Where is the dumpster?' We were then escorted to the dumpster and invited to search its contents. Like brave soldiers we climbed in and began the search.

The top layer of garbage bags was filled with the breakfast remains that had to be sorted through before coming to lunch food. As the heat of the day was re-cooking the scrambled eggs and such, the stench rose and we found it difficult to search

---

[41] I Corinthians 13:1-2

W. Hamp Watson, Jr.

without getting nauseous. We took turns climbing in and out, holding our breath, searching and consoling our friend. Periodically, the dining hall staff would come out to check on our progress. We often heard the words, 'We hope you find it in there. You must be really good friends!'

The search continued and we began to smell and look like the garbage. As I was doing my best to continue searching and fighting the nausea, I began to wonder if the effort was worth it. As I began to doubt, I heard a voice speak 'loud and clear' in my heart, 'Karen, I went through a lot of garbage to get to you, and you were worth it.' Now my tears mixed with the garbage.

After two hours and a half of searching, the retainer was finally found! Yelps and screams were heard resounding from inside the dumpster. The kitchen staff scrambled outside to join the celebration and after they sanitized the retainer in a pot of boiling water, we were back on the road to Richmond Hill rejoicing. Those of us on that trip to Epworth will always sing that line of *Amazing Grace* with a little more insight and enthusiasm, 'I once was lost, but now am found!'[42]

In the category of "Things are not always what they appear to be," comes this story.

My first District Superintendent, Earl Garbutt, told me about his experience with Carlton and Edward Carruth, who were practically identical twins serving churches in our conference. Edward was at Lee Street United Methodist Church in Americus. Earl had scheduled going by to pick him up in his car on the way to a District Meeting. The signal was to be blowing his horn as he pulled up to the front of Edward's Parsonage.

He blew the horn and saw his passenger to be come out on the front porch in his pajamas. He yelled, "Be there in just a minute, Earl!" Then he went back inside.

Not more than an instant later, he came back out on the porch fully dressed and came and got in the car. A miracle? A speed-dresser?

Unbeknownst to Earl, Carlton had come over the night before, and was sitting at the breakfast table in his pajamas. Edward, fully

---

[42] Luke 15

dressed, had finished breakfast. When the horn blew out front, Ed got up to go, but Carlton said, "Wait, Ed!"

Carlton then rushed out on to the front porch in his pajamas, waved at Earl and said, "Be there in just a minute, Earl!"

When he got back inside, he pushed the fully dressed Edward out the front door to get in the car with the astonished Earl Garbutt.

Earl said, "It didn't take me but about a minute to figure out what had happened, but I didn't get it figured out in time to prevent Edward from bursting into laughter. All the way to Cordele, I could picture Carlton, sitting at that breakfast table in his pajamas, with that mischievous glint in his eyes."

Mike Ricker, of "Light for the Nations Ministries," remembers a woman in one of his pastorates:

"Mary was an encourager. She had the capacity to make you laugh at yourself and life, and somehow to believe that no matter how bad things may get, tomorrow would be a better day. She had a body that required an electric lift just to move her around. Her spirit, however, soared unrestrained. She never felt sorry for herself and would not permit you to do so either. I will never forget her telling me the story, between interludes of uncontrollable laughter, of how she decided once to take a shower without anyone's help. She said, 'I got into the shower but I could not get out.'

'Fortunately,' she remarked, 'I had enough sense to carry my phone with me.' She said that she was hesitant about calling 911 because of the embarrassing situation that she was in. She finally decided to call, because she could handle the thought of the EMTs reporting on what they found much better than she could handle the thought of somebody reading the local newspaper headline, 'Fat Naked Woman Found Dead in Her Shower.'

No wonder that her grandchildren adored her. Even though all of them had moved away from the town, they still called and visited Mary whenever they had a chance - or a problem. I cannot remember ever being in her home when one of them, or someone else in need of advice, did not call."[43]

---

[43] Acts 4:36, *A Heart Aflame, pp 25-26*

W. Hamp Watson, Jr.

I also heard Mike tell this one, when I was leading singing as he preached at Tattnall Camp Meeting:

"I can understand, in a simple way, what the Apostle Paul means when he states that we were *'chosen in Christ before the foundation of the world.'*[44] I grew up in a large family. There were nine of us children, four girls and five boys. I was the youngest. In our neighborhood, one of the favorite pastimes of the kids was playing baseball. Nearly everyday during the summer, there was a game going on somewhere. My oldest brother, Butch, would let me go with him when a neighborhood game was forming. I really looked up to him as a hero.

When it came time to choose teams for a ballgame, the same procedure was always followed. First, two captains were selected; then they would choose their team from the pool of possible players on hand that day. Since I was always much younger, smaller and less talented than most of the other kids, it was obvious that I would never, ever, be selected as a captain. Moreover, I also knew that because of my inadequacies, all things being equal, I would likely never be picked at all. If I ended up on a team, I would have to be one of the unfortunate ones who would be left at the end of the selection process and have to hear one of the captains say to the other, 'You can have the rest of em! I've got my team.'

However, when it came time for a big game, as the runt in the bunch, I always seemed to stand a little straighter, feel a little more confident and much less fearful than many of my peers. The reason was because I knew something in my heart. I knew that my elder brother, Butch, was the undisputed best baseball player around. Everyone in our community knew he was the best and acknowledged him as such. I also knew that when it came time for the captains to be chosen at the very beginning, Butch would, without question, be the first to be chosen as captain. I also knew something else in my heart. As great as he was at baseball, he was even better at being a brother. I knew that in spite of my inadequacy, inability, and my weakness, when my elder brother was

---

[44] Ephesians 1:4

W. Hamp Watson, Jr.

chosen as captain, I was also chosen at that moment in him. I was chosen on the basis of his greatness, and his love for me."

Affectionately known as "Wild Bill Kelly" by his contemporaries, W. A. Kelly was an evangelist and one-time Director of Church Extension for the South Georgia Conference of the United Methodist Church. He earned his nickname by incidents like this one.

I was leading singing in the revival as he preached for Austin Wilson at Rebecca. In the middle of his sermon, a dog wandered into the church exciting all the children on the front row as well as taking the full attention of the congregation. Wild Bill halted in mid-sentence as he pointed to a young boy on the front row. He said, "Son, whose dog is that?"

The startled little boy said, "That's Mr. Jones dog."

Wild Bill said, "Well, is Mr. Jones at Church tonight?"

The little boy stood up on the pew and looked all over the congregation. He said, "No, Sir!"

Wild Bill slapped his leg and said, "Well, praise the Lord! He at least had enough religion to send his dog!"

He began preaching again, without missing a lick, with the rapt attention of the congregation.

In one of the meetings when I was leading the singing and Billy Key preached, he told about the man that came down to the altar at the close of every revival service. He had also done that in every previous revival across the years. The burden of his prayer was always the same as he prayed for the power of the Holy Spirit to fill him. He would pray, "O Lord, fill me! Fill me!

But his pastor, who knew his life, on more than one occasion was found on the opposite side of the altar from him. The Pastor was praying just as fervently, "Don't do it, Lord. He leaks! He leaks!"[45]

I think it was also Billy Key that told about the woman that fell into a well. As she was descending, before hitting the bottom, she repented and found the Lord. Upon recovery, always

---

[45] I Corinthians 14:12

W. Hamp Watson, Jr.

thereafter, she would go around pushing people into wells so that they, too, could find the Lord.[46]

It makes sense. Oh, you don't think so?

Bishop Marion M. Edwards, who was elected to the episcopacy from a pastorate at St. Luke United Methodist Church in Columbus, Georgia, tells this story that was treasured in that congregation:

"Before becoming Pastor of First Methodist Church in Atlanta, Pierce Harris was Pastor of St. Luke during depression days. The Board of Stewards met to address a crisis in their finances. Someone made a motion in the Board Meeting that due to the current crisis all payment of Apportionments to the Annual Conference and World Service be suspended. When the Chair put it to a vote there was a resounding chorus of 'Yes!'

The Chair then said, 'All those opposed say "No."'

From the back of the room there came one quiet, 'No.' All eyes turned to focus on D. Abbott Turner, the sole opposition to the motion.

Very quickly, someone who had voted for the motion called for reconsideration of the motion. Another vote was taken and the motion was unanimously defeated. From that day on St. Luke Church has paid all of its Apportionments."

Marion also recalled a story circulating about Pierce Harris, who often played golf with his church members, and others, who were not as circumspect in the language they used on the course. One of his companions said to Dr. Harris, "Pierce, how is it that you can play this game without ever uttering a curse word? I would think you would explode."

Pierce said, "If you look where I spit, I think you'll notice that the grass never grows there again!"

Harry Smith was the pastor at Wesley Oak in Thunderbolt, near Savannah, when a very controversial subject came

---

[46] I Corinthians 14:18-19

up in the Official Board meeting. I think it was back in the days when the John Birch Society and "Dan Smoot Reports" were falsely accusing the Methodist Church of being tainted with Communism. One layman became so incensed at his pastor that, losing it all, he said to Harry, "I'm going to throw you out of the window of this church!"

Harry had a rather high pitched voice that ratcheted up a bit when he was excited. He said, "Well, you may throw me out of that window. But when you get home you're going to tell your wife, 'You know, that preacher didn't want to go out of that window!'"

W hen Superintendent of the Macon District, Cindy Autry, was Associate at Albany First, she recalls:

"In July of 1994, the 'flood of the century' washed through Albany. Unfortunately, our house was in its path (as were thousands of other houses!). Within a few hours, our neighborhood became a lake with only the top halves of houses showing above water. About three and a half feet of extremely dirty water sat in our house for about a week. After that, we all faced the unpleasant tasks of pulling the wet furnishings out of our houses to the street to be hauled away, gutting the interiors, sanitizing the remaining wall studs and floor joists, and rebuilding.

We were out of our house for seven months and moved five times during those months. It was quite an experience from which we learned much!

We learned that when it rains hard continuously for a couple of days, call the U-Haul store to reserve a truck! (We learned this the hard way!!) We learned that for our family, 'things' really aren't as important as we have been told they are. We lost a lot, but for our four-year-old daughter, for example, the two dolls we saved were enough for a time. Family is most important. We learned, or were confirmed in our belief, that the caring of the church family can provide stability in an upheaval in one's life.

We also learned that God works through his people in ways that make all the difference. Volunteers had helped us with the unpleasant task of cleaning out our house. But, they had moved

W. Hamp Watson, Jr.

on to help others. After they left, we learned we had to take up the sub-flooring of the house to insure it would adequately dry out. Our sub-flooring was nailed down with what seemed to be thousands of heavy nails. So, one hot, humid afternoon, Randy and I began prying up the boards using crowbars, while standing in mud that continued to sit under the house. After about thirty minutes, we were exhausted and knew this task was more than we could handle. It would take days for us to do the work alone. That night we went to bed feeling the heaviness of the work before us, and asking God for help, but knowing our volunteers were in other places.

The next morning, when we arrived at the house, a car pulled up with a couple from a United Methodist church in Savannah. They said they had just driven over to help with flood recovery. That morning they had been sent to us. All day, they stood with us in the mucky mire and 98 degree July weather, prying up nailed-down sub-flooring. They were surely the hands of Christ reaching out when we felt defeated. We learned, again, that God uses those of us who make ourselves available in making all the difference for others. We will always be grateful that they made themselves available.

Cindy also remembered: "When our son Darryl was about seven years old, everyday was packed with church work, errands, school events, church events, and more errands. On one particular afternoon, I was under the usual tight schedule as I rushed from work to pick Darryl up from school, stop for a few groceries, run by the laundry, and get home to cook supper before going back to a church meeting that evening. As soon as we drove in the driveway, I hurriedly got Darryl, the groceries, the laundry, and myself into the house.

As I began unpacking the groceries to start supper, I went over my mental list of things to be done. I checked off the list in my mind, making sure I had covered it all. I felt good that I was getting it all done, but I still felt the pressure to keep things moving along.

W. Hamp Watson, Jr.

After a couple of minutes, Darryl walked up behind me in the kitchen. He stood in the doorway and said simply, 'You forgot something!'

I thought, 'How could I have forgotten something? I know I've done everything. Besides, I don't have time to go back and do something else!' The suggestion irritated me, so I turned and with noticeable impatience in my voice asked, 'What did I forget?'

With pure innocence in his voice, bright hopeful eyes, and a slight smile, he said, 'You forgot to hug me!'

He was right. In my frenzy to get things done, I had neglected to do the most important thing of all. Even to this day, my heart aches a little when I remember my neglect.

All around us are people who need the church to reach out and 'hug' them in many different ways. We have to be careful that in doing the needed and necessary things of keeping the church running smoothly and efficiently, we don't neglect to do the most important thing of all—reach out to a hurting world with the embrace of God.[47]

I am thankful for a son who called me back to the thing that mattered most and to a God who blesses every effort we make!"

Index

---

[47] Luke 10:38-42

W. Hamp Watson, Jr.

Nuggets from Near and Far

Evelyn Laycock currently visits her husband, Bill, on a daily basis at a care facility near their home at Lake Junaluska, North Carolina. He's a retired United Methodist Minister. She tells this story about their first day on the job.

"During three years in seminary Bill and I lived in a 17 foot trailer. That length included the hitch. Upon graduation we received our first appointment, five churches that had just been made a new charge. Since there was no parsonage, a three-room apartment was rented for us. We felt like we were in Heaven, having all this space in which to move around.

Soon a knock came on the door. When Bill answered, one of the church members said, 'I'm "Jane Doe". I pay half your salary. If you don't visit whom I say visit and preach what I tell you to preach, I'll not pay you. Here's a jar of blackberry jelly. Welcome to the Circuit.'

When she had gone, Bill turned to me and said, 'Evelyn, we never learned in seminary how to respond to people like this.'

This member would not put her tithe and offering in the collection plate; it might get contaminated. If Bill had pleased her that month, which was seldom, on the fourth Sunday night she would leave the church service early and be standing by the roadside near her home, waving the check in the air. This meant Bill was to stop and get his salary check. She was not out there often.

Another interesting thing "Jane Doe" did was to buy a piano for the church. It was bought under the condition that no one would play it but her. She could not play sharps and flats, so every hymn was played without using any black keys.

Is it any wonder that this church is no longer in existence?

No, we didn't study how to deal with these issues in seminary. We would not have believed such things could happen."

W. Hamp Watson, Jr.

I was leading the singing at Claxton United Methodist Church when I heard Dr. John Church tell about the teenaged girl who came down to the altar during one of his revivals. He said that she was chewing gum as she came—smack, smack. She got to the altar and fell on her knees without a tear, continuing her smacking. As he spoke with her at the altar, he tried to find out why she had come down. He said, "Did you come because you feel that you have sinned?"

She said, "Smack, smack, yep."

He said, "Well, have you confessed your sin to God?"

She said, "Smack, smack, yep."

He said, "Well, what did he say? Do you feel he has forgiven you?"

She said, "Smack, smack, Yep. He said, 'Okey dokey.'"[1]

A young matron joined Dr. Bob Goodrich's church out in Texas, and it wasn't long before she was put on the kitchen committee for the Church Night Suppers. They had a rash of extra dinners to crop up. One night at a big deal at the church, Dr. Goodrich ran into her in the social hall. She was panting, out of breath. He said to her, "How have you been?"

She wiped the perspiration from her brow and said, "I certainly do hope this church can save your soul, 'cause it sure is ruining my health."

The late Bishop Roy Short went into a garage one day to speed up some work on his car. He absolutely had to have it for a trip. The shop was noisy and a fellow named "Doc" was the shop foreman. People were calling him from every direction; machines were humming; hammers were pounding; but in the midst of it all, "Doc" moved around undisturbed. He had a quiet word for every problem that came up; and though there were a dozen others pushing him for their cars, just like the Bishop, he dealt patiently and courteously with each one. Bishop Short said to him, "How do you stand it?"

---

[1] Hebrews 12:18-28

W. Hamp Watson, Jr.

Doc said, "What?"

The Bishop said, "I mean this noise, and all these calls on you. I think I'd go crazy."

Doc said, "Preacher, the Master said, 'Let not your heart be troubled.' And so when I tend to get a little bit irritated, I remember, 'Doc', let not your heart be troubled."[2]

Doc's heart was kept.[3]

Dr. Harry Denman was preaching in Unadilla, Georgia, several years ago. While they were on their way to the little drug store in town for a soda, he suggested to the host pastor that they visit prospects for the church. The preacher said, "Oh we don't have any prospects for church membership here. Everybody in this little town belongs to some church already."

When they went in the drug store, Dr. Denman spotted a teen-aged boy near the soda fountain, and said to him. "Can I buy you a Coke?"

The boy said, "Sure."

Denman said, "Son, where do you go to church?"

The boy said, "I don't go!"

Denman said, "Well, are you a member of any church?"

The boy said, "No, sir!"

Dr. Denman turned to the host pastor and said, "Here's one."[4]

Bishop Kenneth Goodson's daughter was scheduled to go off to college at Duke University. This was back in the days when colleges still tried to be *in loco parentis*, that is, sort of acting in the place of parents as far as discipline was concerned. Her parents received a questionnaire listing things to check that she could do and could not do at college. The Bishop said, "There were things on that sheet that would make my grandmother turn over in her grave." Could she go off on spring break to motels at

---

[2] John 14
[3] Proverbs 4:23
[4] Luke 15:1-10

W. Hamp Watson, Jr.

the beach with male and female students, unaccompanied? You get the picture.

Kenneth said, "I took my red pencil and checked all of them. She can do anything she wants to do."

When she got to college, the Dean called her in. She said, "Is your father off his rocker?"

The Bishop's daughter said, "Some people have said so, particularly preachers in our conference."

The Dean said, "Look at this list. You can do everything on it as far as he's concerned."

The daughter said, "I'm not surprised. He knew which things I'd want to do and which I wouldn't." Then she told the Dean, "When we were fifteen miles from Duke, he said to Mama, 'Aren't there a few things you want to tell your daughter before we get there?'

And Mama said, 'If she hasn't learned them in the last eighteen years, then, this last fifteen miles won't matter.'"

D r. Harry Denman used to head up our Board of Evangelism that was based in Nashville, Tennessee. A woman from Nashville, who had cancer, was in Emory University Hospital in Atlanta. When her nurse looked on her chart and saw that she was from Nashville, she said to her, "Oh, do you know Dr. Harry Denman?"

The woman said, "Yes."

The nurse said, "When I was in High School he came to my home town for a revival and I went down to the altar and after we talked, he gave me this little white Bible. That experience changed my life."

The woman was moved to Duke Hospital in North Carolina. When she got in her room, the nurse looked at her chart and said, "Oh, do you know Dr. Harry Denman?"

"Yes."

"Well, when I was growing up, he came to my home town, and after I joined the church during a Revival, he gave me this little white Bible. I'll always be grateful to him."

W. Hamp Watson, Jr.

She was moved to the cancer research unit at Bethesda, Maryland. When she got in her room and the nurse looked at her chart, she said, "O, do you know Dr. Harry Denman?"

The woman said, "Don't tell me. When you were in high school he came to your town, and you were converted during the Revival he preached, and he gave you that little white Bible you're carrying in your pocket. Right?"

The nurse said, "How did you know?"

But this same Harry Denman came to Screven County, Georgia, to preach a countywide revival. Brother R. E. Harvey was taking him out visiting on the Hiltonia Circuit. They came to a country store where they were going to call on the couple that ran it. The wife was a member, and they hoped to win the husband to the church. This was a dry county in regard to alcoholic beverages, and before they went in, Brother Harvey said, "Dr. Denman, I guess I better warn you. Some people say that these folks sometimes sell a little illegal whiskey."

When they went in, the man was reaching under the counter to put a bottle in a plain, brown, paper bag as he handed it to a customer. The minute Brother Harvey introduced Harry to the proprietor, Harry said to him, "What did you do? Did you just sell him some whiskey?"

After a denial and that rocky start, they finished their visit. But that night, after he got home from the Revival, Brother Harvey's phone was ringing off the hook. He picked it up to hear a woman scream, "Don't you ever bring that man into my store again!"

J. B. Phillips translates Paul in a way that helps us to understand these different reactions to Dr. Harry Denman: *"We Christians have the unmistakable scent of Christ, discernible alike to those who are being saved and to those who are heading for death. To the latter it seems like the deathly smell of doom, to the former it has the refreshing fragrance of life itself."* [5]

Thomas Lane Butts says that when he was growing up in rural South Alabama during the Great Depression, there was an outbreak of hog cholera in their community. One Saturday

---

[5] II Corinthians 2:14-16

W. Hamp Watson, Jr.

afternoon, a group of farmers were sitting around the country store discussing hog cholera. There was one old farmer who seemed to have had more experience than the others; so they turned to him for advice about what to expect. He thought for a moment and then made this encouraging pronouncement: "Hit appears that them what gits it and lingers for a few days, do better than them what gits it and dies right off."[6]

L ong before he was elected as a Bishop from the Florida Conference, Lloyd Knox commuted to Emory's Candler School of Theology. He served a student appointment on the Williamson Circuit out from Griffin, Georgia. As I made that ride to Candler with him for two years, Day and I came to love Lloyd and Edith. He served as a groomsman at our wedding. Lloyd gave me this story:

"The Northern European Central Conference of the United Methodist Church met at the Terminus Hotel in Bergen, Norway, on April 14-18, 1993. There were delegates from Norway, Sweden, Denmark, Finland, Estonia and Russia. Even though my term as president of the World Division was over, I was still a member of the Board of Global Ministries. The Board asked me to be one of its representatives. We needed to elect a Bishop. Bishop Minor from Russia was elected for the first time within the Northern European Central Conference. The delegates were so sure that he was the right choice, that the election took only about fifteen minutes. Imagine that at Junaluska!

Just five years earlier, could anyone have believed that the 'Iron Curtain' would come down in such dramatic fashion?

On Sunday morning, there was a beautiful 'sending forth' service for Bishop Minor at Bergen's First United Methodist Church. For those of us in the chancel area, there was a view of the sky through clear glass. First we saw sunshine and blue skies. Then it rained. Then it snowed. Then the sun reappeared At the end of the service, Bishop Minor said to me, 'These changing climes outside remind me of Russia and the hymn, *Here I Am Lord*, that is so loved by your people back in America'

---

[6] Galatians 6:9

W. Hamp Watson, Jr.

Some of its verses say, 'I the Lord of sea and sky,' 'I the Lord of snow and rain,' and 'I the Lord of wind and flame.'

Bishop Minor and his wife, Gerlinde, never imagined they would be leaders of United Methodism in Russia and Ukraine for thirteen years. Over and over they sang the chorus of that song, *Here I am, Lord,*[7] and at this writing, there are more than one hundred and ten United Methodist Churches in Russia and Ukraine."

J oe Cresson, a columnist for: the *Louisville Courier-Journal*, tells a story about a man in eastern Kentucky, who went to the doctor. As he sat in the doctor's office, he said, he studied the face of a man across the room. "The more I looked at him," he said, "the more I knowed I knowed him. An', what's more, I could tell by the way he was a-starin' at me, he knowed that he knowed me. Well, we set there a-lookin' at each other, knowin' we knowed one another, and finally I decided I was gonna' get up and go over and make sure I knowed him. An' about that time he decided to get up and come over to make sure he knowed me. So we come to the center of the room to make sure we knowed one another, an', you know what? 'Twarn't neither of us!"[8]

A ccording to Dr. Paul Worley, who once raised funds for Candler School of Theology, up in Tennessee at Muncie Memorial Methodist, they were tearing down the old church to make way for a new one. But they had some lovely stained glass windows they wanted to save and put in the new church. One of these was Holman Hunt's masterpiece of Christ knocking on the door of the heart, where the latch on the door is on the inside.

One day while the demolition was going on, Bible school was in session at the church. A junior teacher carried her class of boys and girls into the hull of the old sanctuary where the windows were still in place. They walked through the debris and studied the lovely windows one by one. A sense of awe had begun to come over the

---

[7] Isaiah 6:8
[8] Colossians 3:3

W. Hamp Watson, Jr.

youngsters. Finally, they stopped at Hunt's masterpiece. The teacher said to a little boy, "Johnny, what is the artist trying to depict here?"[9]

Johnny was keen and quick. He said, "That's Jesus, knocking on the door of our hearts."

About that time, a carpenter of the demolition crew had been sent to take down that particular window. He began pecking away with a hammer and a small chisel on the outside of the window.

Johnny said, "Wait! Hush! Be right quiet! You can hear him knocking now!"[10]

At Baxley, Georgia, in 1950, I led singing as Harry Denman preached in the Appling County Revival. We stayed together at Mrs. Ray's Tourist Home directly in front of the church.

I noticed as the week began, that Harry had spilled banana pudding on the front of his black suit as he traveled in the dining car on his way to Baxley. That was the only suit he had with him, and he wore it, without cleaning, for the entire meeting. He did have one change of underwear. He would wash out and hang up the used ones each night to be ready for the next day. His suitcase was filled with little white Bibles to give out to nurses. He also had several copies of *A Testament of Devotion,* by Thomas R. Kelly. He gave one to me and it changed my life.

But several years later, I led singing again as he preached. I noticed that he had a more varied wardrobe—two suits and several shirts and changes, a brighter appearance. I said, "Dr. Denman, you're still traveling light, but you seem to have more variety in your clothing."

He said, "Yes, a good layman taught me something about that. He said to me, 'Harry, why do you keep going around in that one dirty, black suit? Are you trying to show people how religious you are?'"[11]

---

[9] Revelation 3:20
[10] Psalm 46:10
[11] Matthew 6:1

W. Hamp Watson, Jr.

Harry Denman was a bachelor back in the era when the two most popular magazines for Missions put out by the Methodist Church were *The Methodist Woman* and *The World Outlook*. While I was with him at Baxley, Georgia, that week, someone asked him, "Harry, why have you never married?"

He said, "Well, the license costs three dollars, and I never have found a Methodist woman with a world outlook, who had the other dollar and a half."

Bishop Ernest Fitzgerald told about the time the District Preachers and their spouses were meeting at the church where he was serving—Centenary United Methodist Church in Winston Salem, North Carolina. On his way to that meeting, as he walked through the massive stone lined halls, he heard the cry of a child. Following the sound that led him through the massive doors to their chapel, he found a little two-year-old boy futilely trying to push his way out.

He checked the nursery and the preacher party to discover that there was no child missing. They finally all concluded that what they had there was an abandoned child. They called the police and checked the parking lot. A witness recalled a car with a Pennsylvania tag that had sped away from the church. The Congregational Care Committee was called into action.

Reporters came out. The television carried a spot. The newspaper the next day carried a picture of the two-year-old with a story under it, written by one of the reporters. It began, "Someone trusted the Church last night and the Church came through."

The Church did follow through. They were unable to locate the parents. Foster care was arranged and the Bishop said that he had followed the case since he left, and was glad to learn that the child was now well adjusted and doing well in school. "Someone trusted the Church last night, and the Church came through!"[12]

---

[12] Psalm 46

W. Hamp Watson, Jr.

Before he died, I heard John Branscomb tell about a man with one leg in Florida. He and his wife could have no children. It was difficult for them to adopt through the Department of Family and Children's Services. Because of his handicapping condition, more qualified candidates would get any child they hoped to adopt. But finally, a doctor friend called one day, and said, "Jim, come on to the hospital. I think there's a child here that you and Mary can have, if you'd like to have it."

Jim picked up Mary and rushed to the hospital. As he came up to the hospital window where the babies were shown, the doctor stopped him and said, "Jim, you may not want this child. I think I had better warn you, now. The reason it's available is that it was born without one hand."

Jim pushed the doctor aside and looked through the window at the little fellow lying there. He said, "All right, little fellow, you take your one hand and I'll take my one leg and we'll face this world together."

He turned to the doctor and said, "We'll take him, Doc, nub and all."

Could this be the way God takes us... nub and all?[13]

Bishop William Alfred Quayle, of our church, was one of the most unusual and eccentric bishops we ever produced. When he came to retirement, he was getting feeble and he went back to his hometown of Baldwin, Kansas to die. At his home called *Dreamhaven*, he had a rough little house on a crick, and out in the crick he had purposely stuck an old boat with the bottom out of it. In the corner of the yard, he had an old pile of straw to sleep on. At the front of the house there was an old plantation bell, of the type that was once used to call the hands on a farm to dinner. He loved to ring this bell.

He lived alone with his niece, Ella who looked after him and who indulged him in his peculiar interests. A long-time minister friend of his named Parminter also came back there to die. Word came to Bishop Quayle, one day, that his friend had passed on.

---

[13] Psalm 40:6-7

W. Hamp Watson, Jr.

On the day of the funeral he was too feeble to go; he was confined to his bedroom. He looked out on the street of the village and saw the procession assembling for the funeral. He got up enough strength to push up the window and stick his head out. He yelled out to his niece, "Ella, ring the bell!"

Ella didn't want to ruin the solemnity of the assembling funeral procession and so she shook her head at him.

He cried, "Ella, I said ring the bell!"

Knowing his peculiarity and not wanting to upset him unduly, Ella decided she'd have to humor the old gentleman and ring the bell for him, but when she pulled the rope to ring it, she pulled it slowly and solemnly in keeping with the occasion.

When he heard it, the Bishop stuck his head out again, and said, "Ella, **ring** the bell; don't toll it! Ring it! It's Parminter's coronation day!"[14]

It's also interesting that at his own death in 1925; those in charge of **his** funeral rang the bell in his yard.

Index

---

[14] I Corinthians 11:26

W. Hamp Watson, Jr.

Memories from the Manor

Near Christmas at Colquitt, Georgia, I got a complimentary box of matches from Junior Brooks up at his Hardware Store. It had a picture on front of a long-faced, sad looking, doleful bloodhound. Junior said, "That's the way everybody's going to look the first of January."

In contrast, that same year just out of the blue, I got a Christmas card from a woman I didn't even remember. She had just become a resident over at our Magnolia Manor in Americus. She was my "Cradle Roll" teacher, Mary Kendall Jones, daughter of a Reverend Jones who served at Baxley, of whom I said when I was just learning to walk and talk, "I gonna' be preacher like Brother Jones." In the card, were three pages typewritten on a new typewriter given to her by the office staff on her retirement as a secretary in the office at the University of Miami. Obviously, she just wanted to sit down and tell her feeling about life to someone This is one of the things she said in the letter:

"You remember I was deaf when we lived in Baxley. I've been that way since I was ten years old. It doesn't worry me any though. It never has. I get a lot of fun out of everything, and enjoy everything God is kind enough to let me enjoy. It's lots more fun to count the blessings one has than to feel sorry for oneself. I go everywhere I want to go and go it alone, too. It's great fun to sort of watch out for the many kind of lovely things God puts into our lives to enjoy."

A deaf woman living alone, forced to retire because she was over sixty-five, but still doing what she had to do "without complaint"—Miss Mary Kendall Jones, a star that was shining in a dark world.[1]

The Reverend Bill Dupree, who lives in one of the retirement homes on the Campus of Magnolia Manor of Americus, said:

---

[1] Philippians 2:14-15

W. Hamp Watson, Jr.

"One night I had, not a dream, but a nightmare. I dreamed I had died, and my funeral was being conducted. In some odd way I was above, looking down on everything. There was my body in the casket, and my family gathered on the front rows. The minister responsible stood to speak and simply said, 'My mother always taught me, "If you can't say something good about someone, don't say anything."' And he sat down."

Bill also said, "Most persons our age treasure our 'Grand' children. Take a red mental magic marker and circle the 'Grand.' But it works both ways—also 'Grand' parents. Our only grandchild, a granddaughter, Katie, lives in Nashville, Tennessee. At age ten she came to spend two weeks with us in the summer, at Americus' Magnolia Manor.

When I discovered she had never been fishing, I was determined to take her. We loaded up the poles, stopped by a bait place, bought some crickets, and drove out to a friend's farm pond. I would bait the hook; Katie would throw it in and bring in a small brim; and I would take it off the hook and re-bait it. We brought home five fish large enough to fry. We thought she would be thrilled to have a meal of her own fish she had caught. But while her grandmother was frying them, Katie announced, 'Mama Sue, I am not going to eat any of the fish.'

Surprised, Sue asked her why, and Katie responded: 'They have crickets in them!' All of our explaining about cleaning the fish would not change her mind."

Dr. Robert Beckum, Vice President for Church Relations at Magnolia Manor, has only been at the job for a couple of years, while his fund-raising counterpart at The Methodist Home, Dr. Rick Lanford, has been at it for much longer. In fact, Rick has so endeared himself to the people of South Georgia United Methodist churches that they call him "Daddy Rick" just like the children and youth at the homes do. That's quite an accomplishment, to get people to call you an affectionate name, while saying to folks things like this, "I've got good news and bad

W. Hamp Watson, Jr.

news! The good news is that we have more than adequate sums of money to care for all of the needs of all of the residents of the Home for the indefinite future. The bad news is that that money is still in your pockets!'"

So this last year, when the G-8 Summit was scheduled to be at Sea Island, Georgia, and "Daddy Rick" had finagled an appointment as Chief of Chaplains to the event, Robert Beckum said, "I can just envision what's going to happen down there. There'll be a newscast on television of the gathering. The people of South Georgia will be glued to their television screens and see President Bush, Vice President Cheney, and all the heads of the other nations on the platform. Dr. Rick Lanford will be right up there in their midst. These South Georgians will then say to each other, 'Who are all those people up there with Daddy Rick?'"

At the risk of it sounding like a promotion piece for Magnolia Manor, I'm including a story that the Reverend Pledger Parker shared with me. Here are his words:

"In the mid nineteen nineties, I first learned that Magnolia Manor in Macon would have a small number of villa apartments built on campus. 'Wow! It would be wonderful to live there!' I thought. I went to the office to see the administrator.

He welcomed me into his office and invited me to have a seat. I related my interest, that of getting one of the villa apartments that were being built. It was revealed, right off, that there would be only sixteen; and there were lots of people who wanted one. He could not at all assure me of being one of the fortunate few.

'But you will put my name down as wanting one, won't you?'

He felt that he could do that.

Even with little encouragement about chances of getting to live there, gravity seemed to draw me on the path to the Manor campus more and more. Streets were surveyed for the villas. Water, sewer and electric lines were being buried. Drainage culverts were being installed.

The site superintendent's trailer office was set up by the traffic circle and I went by there with my excitement and curiosity showing. 'Can I see what's going on?'

W. Hamp Watson, Jr.

'You can't go on the building site during work hours. After the crew has gone, I have no objection to your looking around.'

The building pads with plumbing in place were being poured. As one was finished and seasoned, the walls began to be raised. Then the next one took shape and the roof of the first one was placed. Four, then eight, then twelve, fourteen, then finally sixteen units became realities.

Occasional visits to the administrator yielded similar advisories. 'I can't assure you that there will be one for you.'

As construction advanced and the facilities really looked like places to live, my wife, Emily, began to go with me. It was usually on Sunday afternoons. By then, others who were assured of being assigned one of the villas were also coming to see them. Joy pervaded the future residents, but **we** dared not 'count our chickens before they hatched.'

Then, one day the administrator said, 'There **might** be a place for you.' There were some who were not ready to give up their own homes. This made changes in the lineup. We had moved up a notch on the list.

The next development was that we might be in the running to get a villa, but we would not have a choice as to which one. We would have to take whatever others did not select. When the final appointments were read, we had more apprehension than we'd ever had before the reading out of our Pastoral Appointments by the Bishop.

The administrator read down to the very last, 'Fourteen to Mr. and Mrs. Doe, fifteen to Mr. and Mrs. Smith, and the sixteenth, Villa 103-D, to Pledger and Emily Parker.' It was the best of them all for our needs and interests.

We moved in on July 17, 1996, and have had nine wonderful years in a community of wonderful, wonderful neighbors! We have no regrets for giving up our home ownership. Thanks be to God!"

Hazel Ansley remembers: "It was promotion Sunday at the First Methodist Church. All the classes were seated with the youngest closest to the front. When it was time for my young charges to stand and answer questions as to what they had learned and then take their seats again, I waited expectantly. I knew, after all my years of teaching Sunday school, that each boy or girl was fully prepared to answer questions on what we had studied. I was beaming, waiting!

To my chagrin, every child said, 'I don't know,' to every question asked. I was bewildered and when we returned to our classroom, I asked them why they had all replied as they had.

Back came a most unexpected response, 'We didn't want to lose you as a Sunday school teacher. We didn't want to be promoted.'

They had to move up anyway, but I was left with a wonderful, wonderful feeling of love."

Evelyn Large, in a bit of memorabilia about a favorite recreation place in the Americus area, tells us in the last sentence of her story why many at Magnolia Manor think she is such a "cool" lady.

"Myrtle Springs is seven miles northwest of Americus, Georgia. Nestled beneath the tall pines and oak trees, to this day the fragrance is still there. Once the center of entertainment for miles around during the late eighteen hundreds and the early twentieth century, it was closed around the middle nineteen-fifties.

Myrtle Springs got its name from crepe myrtle trees, which grew by the flowing spring. The first pool was built with wood near the spring. The children and women went swimming first; then boys and men swam after the women got out. The women in the early twentieth century wore bathing suits down to their feet and to their hands.

The area contained a big bathhouse, a concession stand that we called a store and several cabins. People came in the summertime to camp and enjoy life. The dance hall was built around 1894. It was forty feet by eighty feet and dances were held on Thursday nights, with a band. On Saturdays there was a string band and on the 4th of July people came and stayed all day. Cars parked for miles on both sides of the road and the people walked. The pool was full. We had long rows of picnic tables, always full.

We had reunions, church revivals, and 4-H boys and girls. Boys slept in the barn loft, girls in the camp house. The church baptized in the pool. The camp closed in the nineteen-sixties.

W. Hamp Watson, Jr.

My family moved to Myrtle Springs when I was a little girl. Paul and I bought it in the nineteen-forties and lived there until we moved to Magnolia Manor, Garden Apartment 416.

Cliff Pilcher owns it now and it is kept nice and clean. He has family reunions and church picnics; and I don't have any responsibility for it anymore. But the fact that he owns it doesn't keep me from my memories. It doesn't keep me from going out there either. I go out and just sit and take it all in, so nice and cool."

Merle Lee delights to recall, "When my husband was living, he was the manager of an A&P grocery store in Dawson, Georgia. He had a very good friend, and they were both members of the local Lions Club.

This friend had lots of fun pulling jokes on people. One day he was in the store and two little boys about eight and ten years of age were in there. Mr. Preacher, our friend, said to the boys, 'Do you boys know that I can take my head off?'

They said, 'No sir.'

Mr. Preacher said, 'If I take it off, will one of you hold it?'

One of the boys said, 'No sir!'

The other one was a little bolder. He said, 'Yes sir, I'll hold it.'

Mr. Preacher took both hands and started twisting his head back and forth. He said, 'I'll have to take it off a little at a time.'

What the boys didn't know was that Mr. Preacher had one glass eye. He popped it out, and the two little boys took off running!"

John and Bertha Nell (B'Nell) Bagwell made a carefully planned move to the Americus campus of the Magnolia Manor Retirement Center. Still in good health, they went early rather than later in order to become a part of the community, the church, the city, and the county. Their experience in forty years of pastoral ministry has just been fulfilled the more in that place. For instance, John said:

W. Hamp Watson, Jr.

"Our community is blessed by most interesting and inspiring individuals. Thelma was such a person. She has gone from us now, but we will never forget her. She was in her nineties and confined to her bed. Often she expressed weariness that death would not come. One afternoon B'Nell was visiting her and in the conversation Thelma said, 'I wish that I could die tonight, but I do not want a lot of commotion, like having a heart attack and have everyone come running.'

To this B'Nell replied, 'Then you would like to just die in your sleep?'

With wonderful emphasis, Thelma quickly said, 'Oh, no! I want to be there when it happens!'

I think we all knew what she meant. She didn't want to inconvenience others, but she wasn't going to miss that welcome party for anything!"

John went on to say:
"There is a great appreciation among the residents for our home together. Often, one hears the expression, 'We are family;' and there is a cherished family bond. Charlie gave one of the finest advertisements for Magnolia Manor one morning in our Sunday school class. He was called upon to pray. In his humble, quite eloquent prayer, he said, 'Dear Lord, I'm telling you the truth, this is the best place that we will ever be until we get to heaven to be with you.' Not long after this he entered his heavenly rest, a truly greater place."

Index

W. Hamp Watson, Jr.

Pearls from Our Pastorates

Are you like me in that you sometimes don't accept an invitation because you think the folks don't mean it? The invitation isn't seriously issued. Their invitation isn't real. I don't blame them particularly. It's just the custom. It's a part of Southern hospitality. They issue an invitation, but they don't have any intention of actually having the occasion, or of you showing up for it. I've heard my wife say, "Y'all come and eat with us... just anytime." But if the folks she was asking were to drop in at mealtime to eat, she'd drop through the floor. You have to watch these invitations. There may not be any meal waiting for you.

When I was a single, hungry preacher, a lady said to me, "Come by and eat with me just any time." So I went by one night about suppertime. You know what we had? Rabbit food—lettuce, cabbage, and radishes... stuff like that. She happened to be an officer in the Business and Professional Women's Club. I like rabbit food sometimes, but when it's rabbit food left over from entertaining the B and PW Club the night before; I don't care too much for it.

But some invitations are seriously issued. I remember the night I was at the football game between Rochelle and the Fitzgerald B. Team. It was the first year Rochelle had ever fielded a team, and the whole town had turned out. Day was in the car with Wade, and I had the toddler, Susan, with me on the sidelines. Just before the end of the game, there was a lull in interest, and Johnny Laidler and I got to talking. When the B Team from another school has your team sixty-two to nothing, there tends to be a lull in interest.

Before I could stop her, Susan darted off in the crowd in the direction of the stands... the opposite direction from where our car was parked. I ran after her, but immediately lost sight of her in the push. My heart sprang up into my throat, for just about that time, the whistle blew signaling the end of the game and the mad rush for the cars started. I could see Susan being trampled underfoot, or under the wheel of a car. I started running madly through the crowd screaming at the top of my lungs, "Susan! Susan! I've lost her. Somebody help me find Susan!"

W. Hamp Watson, Jr.

I spotted three of our babysitters, Margaret, Martha, and Boopy, and I put them to work helping me. Then I thought to climb up to the top of the stands to ask the announcer to ask everyone to stop where they were until I could find her. It took him forever to switch on the speaker to say, "Everybody hold still. A little girl has been lost. Help find Susan Watson!"

Pretty soon the word came that she was back at the car with her mother, and my heart came back down out of my throat. She had cut back through the cars, going in the opposite direction from me, and she had found our car.

Do you think that God could ever relax as long as one of God's children is not yet safely home?

I remember standing with three boys from one of my Methodist Youth Fellowships before George Oliver, the Judge of the Police Court in Savannah, Georgia, around 1958. They had been caught stealing fender-skirts. It was their first offence, so far as I knew. I pled for them and told the judge that they were sorry.

He said, "Brother Watson, I know they're sorry; they've been caught. The question is, will they change?"

It was after that that I began to define repentance saying that repentance is not so much being sorry, as it is to stop being sorry.[1]

When we were at Colquitt, Spud and Pat Bush were dear friends. Pat was a Southern beauty that would put Elizabeth Taylor in the shade, and she had a real Southern accent. She told us one day about going down to Tallahassee in the car by herself. As she was leaving the City Limits, she inadvertently ran a stop sign. A police officer pulled her over, came up to the window and said, "Lady, let me see your license."

Pat said, "Oh officer, I came off without my wallet and the license is in it."

The officer said, "Did you know you were driving this car without a tag?"

[1] Mark 1:15

W. Hamp Watson, Jr.

Pat said, "Oh officer, Spud got the new tag last Thursday and was going to put it on, but just hadn't gotten round to it. But it's in the trunk."

Officer said, "Ok, give me your keys and I'll open the trunk and check it out."

Pat said, "Oh officer, I don't have the key. This Chevy is one of those that you can adjust so that you can drive it without the key."

The officer said, "Lady, you're from out of state. You have run a stop sign. You don't have your license; you don't have a tag. You don't even have your key!"

Pat said, "Oh officer, I know you just want to put me under the jail."

He said, "No, I won't this time. Don't turn around. Don't go into Tallahassee. Don't stop anywhere. Go straight home!"

Pat said, "I did drive straight home, and you know all the way home, in my mind, I just fussed at Spud for letting me go off like that."

Ellene Anderson, of the Wesley Monumental Church, told us about her Aunt who lived in another town. On a visit there, her aunt had to go to the bank, and Ellene offered to drive for her.

As they arrived at the Bank, Ellene started to circle through the Drive-through Teller. Her aunt said, "Don't go through there; just pull over here to the side and they'll come out and wait on me."

Ellen did as she was commanded, and sure enough, a teller came from inside the Bank and helped her aunt make all her transactions. Ellene said to the teller, "That's so nice of you to come out and give curb service. I've never seen a Bank do that."

Leaning close so the aunt wouldn't hear, the teller said, "Well, we're really not all that nice. After she had knocked pieces off the Drive-through Teller the third time, we decided it might be cheaper to come out and wait on her."

The valiant little Episcopal Church in Bainbridge hosted a feeding program five days a week for the elderly poor.

W. Hamp Watson, Jr.

They did it so effectively for several years that when they finally had to give it up; the city itself saw the value and necessity of taking over the hosting task. Before we knew that the city was going to take it over, I wondered if our church ought to do it, and I wondered, "How many letters of thanks from the community has the Episcopal church received for providing this site for so long?" Upon reflection I think it was the wrong question. The good works of a church aren't designed to draw attention to it, but as reflected light to bring glory to the Lord of the Church who feeds the hungry with good things.[2]

Sammy Clark, who served as a missionary down in Peru, was there during a terrible earthquake and flood. The Methodist Church had made very little evangelistic impact, but Sammy said, "It came through in a shining hour." For before the Peruvian government, or the World Health Organization of the United Nations, or the U. S. Government, or any other agency had gotten through their red tape, the United Methodist Committee on Relief was there with food and help for rebuilding. It brought a different attitude to the church overnight, for *"If you pour yourself out for the hungry, and satisfy the desire of the afflicted, then shall your light rise in the darkness and your gloom be as the noonday."*[3]

Day doesn't like for me to tell this, but when I was pastor at Bainbridge, one Sunday, Barney Shepard sat down between his wife, Brownie, and my wife, Day, in the Zaidee Slappey Sunday School Class. (Mrs. Zaidee Slappey was Augusta Carruth's mother.) When Day smiled at Barney, he said, "Day, you light up my life!" He had to quickly explain that he'd been listening to Debbie Boone's hit record while working on cars at his shop. So when she smiled, it was on the tip of his tongue. I told Barney that that didn't surprise me, for long before that song was ever written,

---

[2] Matthew 5:14
[3] Isaiah 58:7-10

W. Hamp Watson, Jr.

for over twenty-five years, I'd been singing to her in one way or another—"You light up my life! You give me hope to carry on."[4]

When I went back to Wesley Monumental in January 2001 to help them celebrate their 133rd Anniversary, I told them that I wanted us to try to solve another Savannah mystery, besides the one in *Midnight in the Garden of Good and Evil*. That mystery was, "Why Wesley Monumental?" Now, I wasn't focussing on the name of the church, Wesley Monumental, as interesting as that is. You've heard that story.

The church was referring to itself with a much less pretentious name, "Wesley Memorial". But the Savannah Morning News called it Wesley "Monumental", since it was to be a monument to the Wesleys, John and Charles, and the name stuck. It was fun to be pastor of that church and get the advertising mail. I remember I got one offer of a great purchase of land down in Florida somewhere, and the letter began:

Wesley Monumental
429 Abercorn Street
Savannah, Ga.

"Dear Mr. Monumental":

But more than the mystery of its name is the larger mystery. Why is there a Wesley Monumental at all? In the aftermath of a destructive civil war when people were scrambling just for places to live and food for their tables, why did these people undertake to build a great cathedral? Why did they do it? This is another Savannah Mystery.

Several years ago when I was District Superintendent of the Savannah District, I was out at Wilmington Island United Methodist Church on a Communion Sunday morning. I was just dropping in unannounced to see how things were going in that congregation and to hear their preacher. I got a bonus. It was

---

[4] Matthew 5:14

W. Hamp Watson, Jr.

during the time that Hershell Walker was doing his heroics at the University of Georgia. The Bulldogs had been declared national champions. During the children's sermon, the pastor, Jim Jensen, threw open his black robe to reveal underneath a Red and Black T-shirt with the caption emblazoned—"WE'RE NUMBER 1!" This brought a huge laugh from the congregation. Later at Communion as he broke His body for us and shared His blood with us, Jim showed us who was really Number One.

How did He get to be Number One? Was it by battering brutally through the line? Did he overpower his opponents with crushing force? Paul just says, *"Through Him God was pleased to reconcile to himself all things, whether on earth or in heaven, by making peace through the blood of his cross."* He's Number One in vulnerable, dying love for others, so that in him, all things might hold together.[5]

On a vacation I was walking on the beach early one morning and saw twenty-nine pelicans fly over in perfect formation. I counted them. A little bit later, I saw one lone pelican against the sky. It made me think about the time that William Cullen Bryant saw a waterfowl winging its way against the western sky just at sundown. He followed it on "its solitary way" until the "abyss of heaven" had "swallowed up its form", and he said:

He, who from zone to zone,
Guides through the boundless sky thy certain flight,
In the long way that I must tread alone
Will lead my steps aright.

I Remember how in one Thanksgiving sermon at Wesley Monumental, I told about being raised in Baxley, Georgia, with a mentally ill father and a mother who died after a double mastectomy, when I was just sixteen. I told how I sold papers at the hotels at six o'clock in the mornings, from the time I was ten years old, to help make ends meet. But the ends would keep growing farther apart. When I finished that little recital, Cecil

[5] Colossians 1:15-20

W. Hamp Watson, Jr.

Abarr, the local head of the Branigar Corporation, came up to me afterward, and said, "Hamp, you want to have a contest on telling 'poor' stories? I can match you story for story."

And the truth is that nearly all of us remember the quarry from which we were dug.[6]

A lady from one of my churches went shopping. She distractedly left her purse with about a hundred dollars and all her credit cards in the lounge. It was sometime before she remembered it, and when she did, her husband, who was with her, said, "You'd just as well forget that money and start notifying your card companies. It's gone now."

She went back and searched frantically for it. Sure enough, it was gone. But before leaving the store she decided to check at customer service, and to her amazement, her purse had been turned in with money and cards intact. As the husband told me about it, you could see that he could still hardly believe that somebody had been a star shining in a dark world.[7]

A cross the years, I've had members who had to make military or business moves and had the unpleasant task of trying to sell their houses. It's been particularly tough in small towns or rural communities. There are just not that many buyers. It made me think of the small boy that Allen Funt talked to on Candid Camera one night. He said his Daddy was trying to sell their house. But, he said the whole family was discouraged because houses were hard to sell and they didn't have a buyer yet. But the little boy said that his Daddy would always say, when they failed to sell it, "Fink of Fafe!"

Allen Funt didn't understand what the little boy was getting at at first, but finally saw that he was saying that they must have faith that they would be able to sell their house. It came out with him, "Fink of Fafe!"

---

[6] Isaiah 51:1
[7] Philippians 2:15

W. Hamp Watson, Jr.

Then, Allen Funt asked him, "What would you do if you wanted to get a million dollars?"

The little boy said, "Work!"

Our life's partner is under threat of death in the middle of the night with serious surgery. We commit ourselves to the outcome, like a little English lady member of mine who had a husband with a blood clot on his brain requiring the scalpel. She said, "Worst things happen at sea!" I'd never heard that quaint English phrase, "Worst things happen at sea." But like her, we find that the master of the wind and the waves is adequate to sustain us whatever the outcome.

Ella Lewis was our cook and childcare person, who saved our lives when Day and I were serving the five point Rincon Circuit and had three little stair-step children. It wasn't your typical master-servant relationship. She didn't have to work; she just saw the weariness in Day's eyes and couldn't turn us down. Her husband, Corley, had a good job at Union Camp Paper Corporation, and when our larder got low, Ella would bring us steak out of her freezer. She was telling Day that she was in charge of purchasing the organ for their little church, and a woman said to her, "Ella, you know there are a lot of people in this church that are upset with the way you're handling this organ thing." Ella said, "You tell 'em I'm not working for them."

Dr. Anthony Hearn, at the Effingham Camp Meeting, called for volunteers from the young people to put up lights in the tabernacle, and he only got one or two half-hearted volunteers. But then he called for volunteers to undertake the dangerous job of getting rid of the wasp nests in the preachers' tent that had frightened the preachers. A whole raft of teen-aged boys responded. They wouldn't volunteer for the easy and unexciting. They wanted the challenging and dangerous.[8]

---

[8] I Samuel 17:31-32

W. Hamp Watson, Jr.

The five-year-old granddaughter of one of Day's best friends came home from Sunday school where the Baptism of Jesus had been illustrated, even with pictures of a real dove descending. She said to her grandmother, "Grandma, when you were baptized, did the dove come down on you?" Jane said, "Well, Darlin', I don't think so."

Her granddaughter said, "Did for Jesus!"[9]

Since I was about eight or nine years old, I have loved and recited Sidney Lanier's poem, *"The Marshes of Glynn"* because my Daddy loved it so. He knew it by heart from the beginning to the end. I once drove a bus to take some older adults on a trip to Epworth-by-the-Sea and drove under those mossy oaks. The sight of those oaks made me wax eloquently, saying,

> Beautiful glooms, soft dusks in the noon day fire,
> Wildwood privacies, closets of lone desire,
> Chamber from chamber parted with
> wavering arras of leaves,
> Cells for the passionate pleasure of prayer
> for the soul that grieves.

Those old folks thought their pastor had gone crazy up there driving that bus.

But there's another part of that poem that I never fully understood, until that trip to Epworth. It's the part that goes:

> As the marsh hen secretly builds her nest on the watery sod,
> Behold I will lay me ahold on the greatness of God.

Do you know how the marsh hen builds her nest? I didn't. Mary Nell Waite, in the Museum at Epworth, told us. She said, "The marsh hen weaves her nest around the deep rooted marsh grass in such a way, that when the tide comes in, the nest rises and falls with the water." So whether the tide is in or the tide is out, whether the tide is high or the tide is low, I build my nest on the

---

[9] Mark 1:9-11

W. Hamp Watson, Jr.

greatness of God, whose roots reach down to the soil, and regardless of the tide, I am secure in the greatness of God.[10]

To explain to me why he didn't want me calling on him to lead in public prayer at Rochelle Methodist, Pitts Culpepper said, "Up at my home in Greenville, Georgia, a new preacher called on a prominent lawyer, who had never prayed in public, to lead the prayer. He looked around to see if there was anyone close enough that he could nudge to pray in his place, but finding nobody, he started off. He prayed a pretty good prayer, but toward the end, he said, 'And oh God, let the farmers make a good crop so they can pay the merchants, so that everybody will have money to pay the preacher, whose duty it is to pray. Amen.'"

My Summer Associate, Sammy Clark, and I went up to the Rochelle Church to clean up after Youth Activities Week. One of the things that made the week so wonderful was a giant cross, flood-lighted each night in the worship center, so that the shadow was cast high on the wall of the church, overshadowing us all. But Sammy and I took the cross down. We stored it down in the stairway that led to the water-filled basement back in 1957. For Jesus, they compelled one Simon of Cyrene to bear his cross; but early that morning; Sammy Clark compelled one Hamp of Rochelle to help carry it down the basement stairs.

But do you see what Sammy and I did? We're guilty of the crime. We took the cross down in the church. This is why it's hard for people to come under a healing shadow now. I guess that's how it happened, because today, everything else under the sun is talked about in the church:

- The fact that religion will give you peace, poise and power, solve all your problems and heal all your diseases,
- Having a church in town is good for business and makes a healthy community,
- You'll succeed in business if you play fair and keep the golden rule,

---

[10] II Corinthians 1:15-22

W. Hamp Watson, Jr.

- You better get ready for the "rapture". As the bumper sticker I saw the other day put it, "In the event of the Rapture, this car will be driver-less."

But the cross fades into the distant background, as far out, out-of-sight, and forgotten as that cross down in that water-filled basement.[11]

I watched one day with an old man as construction was underway on the social hall behind his little church. I knew his wife was dead; his family had moved off. But he had put a lot of money into the building; and he was out there every day to watch the construction. I said to him, "Mr. Des, why are you so interested in this building?"

He said, "When I came along, somebody had put this church here for me. I guess I'm just paying my debt to them by leaving something for somebody else."

We pay our debt to the past by obligating ourselves for the future, in the present. As Bishop John Owen Smith used to say, "It's our time!" For yesterday is but a dream, and tomorrow is only a vision, but each today, well lived, makes every yesterday a dream of happiness, and every tomorrow a vision of hope.[12]

When I think about the last big church I served, Wesley Monumental in Savannah, I wonder. Suppose the old man, Cornelius Rogers, Sunday School Superintendent at old Trinity Church, had not been a dreamer. When he tried, right after the Civil war, to get an outpost Sunday School going in a room at Chatham Academy, the man on the committee with him, who was supposed to fix up the room, failed to get it ready. When Rogers asked him why, he said, "Because I have other fish to fry." So Rogers himself had the room furnished, and under the leadership of the Associate Pastor at Trinity, the class was bursting the seams of the room. The Associate, Cox, got discouraged and said he

---

[11] Mark 8:34
[12] Acts 2:17

W. Hamp Watson, Jr.

couldn't do satisfactory work in just a room. The German Lutherans had abandoned a little coffee pot shaped church on the back of a lot facing Drayton Street, and it was available, even though it was full of holes shot through the roof by Union Soldiers who had slept in it. But there was no money in 1867 to buy the little church.

Rogers said to the Board at Trinity, "I'll give fifty dollars toward repairing the little church."

Robert McIntire spoke up and said, "I don't think Brother Rogers is able to give so much, but I will give one hundred dollars."

Brother Walker said, "I will see you Bob, with another hundred." And the members of the Board kept on subscribing until they had run the amount up to eight or nine hundred dollars.

McIntire finished out what was needed, and Rogers said, "Brother Cox moved his mission in, which I think had about seventy members, and everything went on splendidly." There's so much more dreaming and doing to the story, but that was the beginning of Wesley Monumental Church.

When I was serving Wesley Monumental in Savannah, the missionaries that church supported came back in 1989 from Africa for a relational and promotional visit. It was my first time to know Doctors Ellen and Jeffrey Hoover and their children Jane, Jeremy, and Mark. They showed us slides of a land of abject poverty. They were working constantly in education in that land so hungry for learning and for worship.

Some of us, knowing that they both had PHDs from Yale, thought about how much higher a standard of living they would have been able to afford if they had just stayed over here with us. So, somebody asked them, "How do you stand it?" We were overwhelmed at the contrast of our plenty and their poverty in almost every materially measurable scale of living.

They were kind to us in their answer. They said, "We have some compensations. We have no washing machines, but we have washerwomen who are available; and we really feel an obligation to use them since there's an 80% unemployment rate. We also have a

W. Hamp Watson, Jr.

faithful maid for childcare." But we all knew the deeper answer they could have made. It was the thing we sensed in them that made us hunger for something we might not fully have.

They had "blessings"—riches, not measurable on any standard of living scale. They had that freedom from measuring their worth on the standard of living they were able to afford. They weren't threatened if they weren't able to stay up with their peers in housing. They weren't concerned that they didn't live in a section of some city that made a statement about their status. They didn't seem to worry that they couldn't send their children to the best schools, so they could marry the right persons, to get ahead in the rat-race of affluence. They told the church about the harrowing circumstances of danger and persecution that they had faced since they had last seen them. But somehow, we sensed that they were not victims. Through it all, they were Kingdom People, experiencing the blessings of God.[13]

S ome years ago I turned the corner to go to the church with a mechanic who was bringing me back before he took my car to work on it. We saw the schoolyard and the children on their way to their classes. He said, "They don't know it, but they're having their happiest days, ain't they, preacher?" Oh we all say something like this at one time or another, but isn't it sad when your work makes you long for earlier more irresponsible days?

A tragedy comes in a family, like the mother who interrupted my prayer after the death of her five-year-old with bulbar polio to ask, "Why did God let this happen to her?" I was crushed with her, sharing her grief, and silent I think. But in the next few days there were those well-meaning friends who dropped by with ready answers. Mrs. Itcud Benworse came by. So did Mr. Ujust Gottatakit. Mrs. Uwill Learnalesson dropped in. But the worst one was Mrs. Itwas Godswill. Jesus did no such shallow counseling that insulted the sufferers and maligned God.[14]

---

[13] Matthew 5:1-11
[14] Deuteronomy 29:29

W. Hamp Watson, Jr.

A High School boy, in a church I served, told me that he was thinking about going into the ministry. He said to me, "Hamp, if God let's me win the District Declamation Contest next week, it'll be a sign to me that he wants me to go into the ministry."

That boy was about as unfitted for the task as anybody I knew, so with some concern,, I asked Sammy Clark, who was serving that summer as my Associate Pastor, about him. I said, "Sammy, Joe says that if God lets him win the District Declamation Contest next week, it'll be a sign to him that God wants him to go into the ministry. What'll we do?"

Sammy said, "Let's pray for him to lose."

"You are not to put the Lord your God to the test."[15]

There are at least three of us old men in the Glenwood Hills United Methodist Church that have computers and are on the Internet; and we've discovered that the people in this sort of business haven't given up. Have you heard about SPAM on the Internet? That's when a message that you don't want to come up on the screen just bombards you with an advertisement and you can't get the thing to go off so that you can do the thing you wanted to do. SPAM has assaulted Dub Simmons, our Minister of Music, Bill Trobaugh, our volunteer Associate Pastor, and me.

One day, Dub's wife, Nina, heard a report on the television that said some of the SPAM circulating had a virus in it. Later that day, Nina reported to Dub that she had found some "Spam" in their pantry and she wanted to reassure him that she had thrown it all out.

When Bill and Dub and I open our computer screens, there it is—SPAM—an ad wanting us to respond to this dating service. It'll match us up with some attractive woman, just fitted to our needs. They don't know that between us, we've been married to the same women for over one hundred and sixty-three years.[16]

---

[15] Matthew 3:7
[16] Matthew 19:6

W. Hamp Watson, Jr.

An alcoholic came to see me in my study one day. He'd been drinking since his teens, was now over fifty, and still drinking. He said to me something like this. "Preacher, I knew you was a good man, so I've tried everything else. I decided I'd try God to see if he could cure me of my drinking problem." We spent about an hour together that day. I suggested AA, but he didn't follow up on that. He never came back to see me. The next time I saw him I could tell he'd been drinking and I asked him why he hadn't come back.

He said, "Well, I came that day, and it didn't do any good, so I figured religion wouldn't be any help."

He spent thirty years getting in that condition and he was greatly disappointed because God didn't extricate him in an hour. This is "unfaith" clamoring to be coined to "faith" by proof. It's trying God instead of trusting him.[17]

When Miss Helen Rosser, Missionary to Korea, spoke at our Colquitt Methodist Church, she told about being on the Korean Death March, in which fifteen hundred prisoners were made to walk over rough terrain. There was a particular valley through which they went in the deep of winter. There they lost about half of their number to exposure and malnutrition. She said, "They had taken away our Bibles, so the only way we could keep our spirits up was to sit around, when the guards were inattentive, and share with each other from memory all the Scripture passages we knew. Think how often we said, 'Yea though I walk through the valley of the shadow of death!' That was our valley of the shadows."[18]

Their harshest treatment came from a Communist Captain, who took it as his personal task to brainwash Helen. He would scoff at her faith and try to humiliate her in every way that he could. Helen said, "I would say under my breath, 'I will fear no evil, for thou art with me.'" She'd rebuff him with kindness. I remember after these forty years that diminutive, sweet-faced little woman saying, "You know, I could hardly believe it, but one day

---

[17] Matthew 3:7
[18] Psalm 23

W. Hamp Watson, Jr.

that Captain said to me, 'Miss Rosser, could you help me to know your God?'" The brain-washer wound up being, "Washed in the Blood of the Lamb."

Off in a revival at Woodstock, out visiting with the preacher, Harry Alderman, we went by the hospital so he could check on a member, who had just given birth to a baby after a long, perilous incubation period. She'd been down for three months before birth, unable to do anything at home. The husband had to do his work and hers, and was getting over an accident himself. While we were in the room, a dozen roses arrived from the husband, and as she looked at the card, Harry thought about the husband's injury and said, "How's your husband?"

She looked up and said, "Oh, he's wonderful!" She was smiling through tears of joy.

Harry never did find out about the husband's health that day. But we both found out about the health of that marriage.[19]

I was counseling a couple one time and the husband said, repeating the old saw we all have heard, "Every time we have a disagreement, she gets historical." He didn't say hysterical, he said historical. He said she remembered everything he had ever done wrong and could catalog it with date and time and place. She did a little of that in our session. They both needed to start keeping no record of wrongs. Paul said, love *"Never looks back."*

But it can be the man who is paranoid about faithfulness. I counseled a couple in which the man mistrusted his wife for no reason. All I could do was ask her to recognize his weakness by always checking in with him when they were apart to quiet his mind's imaginings. He had had a failed marriage from infidelity. And I told him to flex the muscles of trust. Stop quizzing her. Stop checking on her. *"Always look for the best."*

I've had a lot of failures in counseling, but the warmth with which they greeted me when I ran into them at a funeral thirteen years later told me that something worked that time.[20]

---

[19] Ephesians 5:21-33
[20] I Corinthians 13

W. Hamp Watson, Jr.

Y ou might think that going down to the store to buy a box of Morton's Salt was a quite American thing to do, if you had not had the experience I had sometime back. I helped Charlie Jackson in a meeting in Brunswick; and the Brunswick Harbor Pilot carried Charlie and me with him on a trip to take the *Cecile Erikson* out to sea. The U.S. Corporation, Morton Salt Company, owned this ship. It was built in Japan at a cost of one and a half million dollars. It flew under the Liberian Flag to avoid payment of U.S. taxes. It had a Liberian crew to avoid the high salaries that had to be paid to unionized American seamen. It had a Norwegian captain and a first mate from the Bahamas. But American ship designers designed it. All this to get salt on your table. Everyone is my neighbor.[21]

O ne of the Boykin twins, who was eight years old out at Bethesda Church in Effingham County, was talking to his grandmother about heaven. He said, "Grandma, will people know each other in heaven?"

She said, "We don't know all the details but we certainly hope so."

He thought about that a minute and then said, "Will Charles Zettler be there?" Charles Zettler was a school classmate that rode the bus with him and had given him a pretty hard time during the year. He said, "Will Charles Zettler be there?"

Again, not knowing quite what to say, his grandmother said, "Well, I hope so!"

The twin said, "Well, I don't want to go then."

V ictory Drive leads through Savannah out to Tybee Island and is lined with palms and beautiful azaleas. Bonaventure Cemetery is north of it, bordering the Savannah River.

Mrs. Mary Pollard, of the Wesley Monumental United Methodist Church, had lost a friend named, Laura. The Rev. Ernest Seckinger, from the Cokesbury pulpit, said at her funeral, "When we leave the church here, the funeral procession will soon

[21] Luke 10:25-37

W. Hamp Watson, Jr.

cross over Victory Drive. So it is with Laura. She has just crossed over Victory Drive!"

Mary Pollard took that phrase and came up with this rhyme:

As the preacher read the book divine,
I whispered, "Dear Lord, these words of thine
Are so comforting to our hearts
When from this earth a loved one departs."

'Twas then we heard the preacher say,
"The funeral cortege along the way
Will soon cross over Victory Drive."
It's true of Laura. She's alive!
She's just crossed over Victory Drive.

Hallelujah! She crossed over there
Without the aid of her wheel chair!
For this, oh God, I glorify you--
That our bodies are all made new.
Mortal puts on immortality.
Death is swallowed up in victory.
Praise God, our Laura is alive!
She's just crossed over Victory Drive.[22]

In Wesley Monumental Church, when sixteen of our families pledged large amounts at the Steering Committee pledge service, one of our leaders told us why he was a committed giver today. As a little child—six or seven or eight—the family was faced with a crisis. They didn't have enough money to get clothes and some of the other things they thought were necessities, and child that he was, he spotted a big roll of bills in his mama's pocketbook. He said, "What do you mean we don't have any money? Look at all that money."

But his mother said, "Hush! That's the tithe.[23] That's the Lord's. That's already committed to the church, and it's going Sunday."

---

[22] I Corinthians 15:53-56

W. Hamp Watson, Jr.

And our leader said, "That left a profound impression on me, and I don't ever remember after that making a conscious decision to tithe. When I got my own income, it just seemed to be the right thing to do."[24]

In my early ministry, I'll never forget how I was brought up short one day in a hospital room, when I asked the man on the bed if he'd like for me to have prayer. He said, "If you think it'll do you any good, go right ahead." That maybe was a rude thing for him to say, but I needed it. I needed it to keep me from ever just going room to room because that's what I thought a preacher was expected to do.

I was called back to Pitts, Georgia, to have the funeral of a thirty-seven year old wife and mother of two little boys, who died with leukemia. As I rode toward Pitts I remembered Ruth King's story. When she married Robert, she was timid and shy, almost to the point of being a recluse. But her mother-in-law, Titter King, taught the primary class at Pitts Methodist and did all she could to encourage her to come to church and get out and be with people. It was seven years before Ruth joined the church after the Spring Revival before I went to Pitts as Pastor in June. That June I persuaded her to become MYF counselor, and with fear and trembling she took it.

I watched a transformation that year. The timid, shy recluse became an outgoing, friendly person who won the love of over thirty young people. As I rode I thought of her mother, Mrs. Hatcher, whom I remembered as more withdrawn even than Ruth in her earlier days. She lived about four miles from Seville Methodist; and I remembered how Mary Nell Sargent drove by week after week, trying to interest Mrs. Hatcher in life and the church, but so far as I knew she was still a withdrawn, lonely person. I wondered how she would take this crushing blow, with no more resources than she had to draw on. When I got to Pitts, I discovered some things. The friends poured it out to me.

---

[23] Genesis 28:20-22
[24] I Peter 2:21

W. Hamp Watson, Jr.

Through all her terminal illness, Ruth never once complained, or doubted God, or cursed her fate. Never once did she ask, "Why did this have to happen to me?" Numbers testified that they dreaded going to see her in the hospital because they knew her situation, but they were always glad they did, for rather than having to give help they received it. Her thoughts were never for herself but always for her husband and children whom she gave into God's hands, even as she surrendered up her own life unto him.

When she was given the choice of returning home, or of giving herself to research to combat leukemia at Emory Hospital, she chose to stay at the hospital if it would ever offer any hope of help to someone else.

Her family was quiet and controlled, even natural with some warmth and wit, as they talked of her going. The biggest surprise was her mother, whom I had expected to see crushed and broken beyond recovery. I discovered that Mary Nell Sargent's persistence had finally prevailed; and Mrs. Hatcher had for several years now been an active member at Seville Methodist.[25] With her church friends close around her, she spoke calmly and radiantly of Ruth's going.

When I was a boy, some of my buddies and I got into a pea-gun war in the neighborhood on a Sunday afternoon. We got carried away and darted into the Baxley Methodist Church. There we hid down behind the pews to shoot our little green berries through our hollow bamboo reeds at each other. Those pews simulated a great fort to hide behind. When the folks came into church that night, they squashed the little green berries into the new carpet. What a mess! Dr. Long, the local druggist and the Lay-leader, saw me looking sheepish. He said, "Hampton, you had something to do with this, didn't you?"

The upshot was that he agreed not to tell my mother, **if** I'd get the rest of the boys and try to clean it up. For him to have told my mother would have been a fate worse than death. She was the castor oil lady and the "thin little peach switches" lady. But he forgave me and I didn't have to meet that fate.

---

[25] II Timothy 4:5

W. Hamp Watson, Jr.

Years later, when I was pastor at Rochelle, they caught some boys who had shot out windows in the church with their BB guns. They had them by the napes of their necks before me. Somehow, for the life of me, I couldn't help but forgive them and refuse to press charges as we worked out a way that they would replace the windows.[26]

When I went over to Liberty Hill Church in Wilcox County as their young student pastor, some of the old folks didn't want to change the time for the annual Revival, which hit at the same time that I was in school that summer. The Lord had always visited Liberty Hill the third week in July, which was "laying by" time, and many of them thought that he couldn't come any other time. But I remember Old Brother Lon Connor, a layman then in his eighties, standing up in the meeting. He said, "Times change, boys. We've got a preacher that needs to finish his education. Anybody that's heard him preach ought to agree to that. I think we ought to move the revival to August, when he can be with us."

He was the oldest man there, but the most progressive in thought—a formed but not a fixed character. His humor carried the day and we moved the revival to August—or maybe it wasn't humor.

I remember a tenant farmer family with five children. The father was the lay-leader in the most country of my five country churches on that circuit. Day and I thought they couldn't afford it, but they'd have us come eat with them after church. He'd look at that table full of simple, Southern cooking with my four and his seven gathered round it, and with a twinkle in his eye he'd say, "Now you see what it is. If you're a mind to eat it up from me and the chillun', just take out and help yourself." I wasn't surprised in later years to discover that the little eleven- year- old daughter who played the piano for the worship services at their church became the editor for the magazine "*Engage-Social Action*" for the

---

[26] I Peter 4:10

W. Hamp Watson, Jr.

Board of Church and Society for the entire United Methodist Church. In a letter at Christmas, she told how she and her husband, with their church, had just finished building their fourth house for Habitat for Humanity.[27]

I knew a man who was the father of three boys in one of my MYFs. When I had dinner with them in their home, his boys were as quiet as lambs. They spoke in subdued tones when they answered their Daddy, and it was always "Yes, Sir" that they said. But these boys were literally Holy Terrors at MYF. They were destructive. They tore up the chairs and tables and damaged the concrete block walls.

But, I could sort of understand this great contrast. I knew this man was the father of an illegitimate child in one of my other churches on that charge. These boys feared the belt their Daddy wielded. He would use it with the buckle end. But they basically knew the stuff from which he was made. They knew he had no real claim to make against them whenever they played fast and loose with any of their responsibilities to others in life.

We can joke about killing over the quota in front of our children, about that time we outwitted the traffic cop, but then, try to get respect for our desire that they not break laws or cheat at school.[28]

Wesley Monumental Church in Savannah, Georgia, owns a beautiful retreat center called Wesley Gardens, out on Moon River. The name of the river was changed from "Back River" to "Moon River" when a Savannah native wrote a beautiful song by that name.

Moon River, Wider than a mile,
I'm crossing you in style some day.

Anyway, while serving there I learned that back in 1927, a real estate development firm in Savannah failed; and investors lost

---

[27] III John 1-8
[28] Luke 2:50-52

W. Hamp Watson, Jr.

some $300,000. No corruption was involved by the man who had founded the firm, but one of the tragedies was that The Union Society, which supports the Bethesda Home for Boys founded in 1740 by George Whitfield, was one of the biggest investors in the certificates offered by this failed realty company.

What happened after 1927, of course, is well known to everyone. The firm couldn't get back on its feet. But because the president of the firm was a faithful Christian, the situation weighed heavily on his chest, so heavily that some said it hastened his death. In 1957, thirty years after the financial collapse, this man's son deposited in the Chatham Savings Bank enough money so that every investor or his/her heir was paid back the original investment. The Union Society and Bethesda Home for Boys shared in that windfall which no one had ever expected. For, you see, they didn't count on somebody like Johnny Mercer, who then lived in Hollywood, to listen to the voice of the King who was glad to be called, "The Lord is our Righteousness."[29]

A s a youth, Raymond McKinney witnessed back at his little country church, Kramer, after he'd seen the light at Dooly Camp Ground. He said, "I learned that while it may be good, going to church and sittin' in a pew ain't any more gon' make you a Christian than settin' in a hen house is gon' make you a chicken!"[30]

I n a former church I was teaching a Bible study. Two of the women were disturbed when they ran across God saying, *"I the Lord your God am a jealous God, punishing children for the iniquity of the parents, to the third and fourth generation of those who reject me."*[31] Did that ever bother you?

We decided that the writer wasn't thinking of our good, loving God as one who would punish little innocent children, who couldn't control how their parents behaved. He was just expressing a principle that's so true—if parents reject God, if parents neglect

---

[29] Jeremiah 23:5-6
[30] Matthew 7:21
[31] Deuteronomy 5:9

W. Hamp Watson, Jr.

and abandon their children, if alcoholism runs rampant in one generation, so often it damns the next. You sow a thought and you reap an act, sow an act and you reap a habit, sow a habit and you reap a character, sow a character and you reap a destiny. But still, "Is anything too wonderful for the Lord?" God is able to break even that cycle.

Since we were in a church where Dr. Edwin Chase had served for eleven years as Minister of Counseling and Cultivation, we had to think about his story:

- how Edwin came out of a dysfunctional family and wound up after neglect and abandonment at the Methodist Home for Children and Youth in Macon,
- how he was sent to college and seminary by the Home and all us South Georgia United Methodists,
- how he served several years as counselor at the Pastoral Institute in Columbus,
- how he came back home to Macon to head up the Family Institute on the grounds of the Children's Home,
- and, to top it all off, in addition to all this he is now the coordinator and the Chief Pastoral Counselor for all the Pastoral Families in the South Georgia Conference of the United Methodist Church.

This child of dysfunction is the one who keeps all of us preachers functioning. Every time Edwin thinks about that he laughs. "Is anything too wonderful for the Lord?" No! "For nothing will be impossible with God." "What is impossible for mortals is possible for God."[32]

I was helping in a meeting in Woodstock, Georgia, when the preacher and I went to see an old man who had been living in the community for twenty years. This man had never joined the church. The preacher finally raised the question about his church membership with him, and seeking to understand him he said, "Maybe you've just been a little bit timid about standing up in front before a crowd to join. Is that it?"

---

[32] Mark 10:26-27

W. Hamp Watson, Jr.

The old man's wife who was sitting there said, "Timid! Yes, he's timid! When we went to get married, we went to the parsonage, and Ollie's knees were shaking so bad that he couldn't get out of the wagon. I asked him if he still wanted to go through with it, and he said he did. So we had to get married sitting in the wagon. We asked the preacher to come out and he married us right there, sitting down."

I became deeply concerned for a dear friend of mine who lost his wife with cerebral cancer. Ten years earlier, she'd had brain surgery to remove a tumor, and though the chances were very slim, she miraculously recovered, living ten more years gratefully and graciously. She blessed the lives of all that knew her by her attitude in suffering. But in the last stages of this illness that finally killed her, a group of friends, that were in a healing prayer group, came to both her and her husband with the implied message that they just didn't have enough faith or the wife would be healed.

When she was dead, they were still dogging the husband with this half-baked, misguided theology. Forgetting the lifetime of service of this man in his church in every large or small office he could hold, forgetting the miracle of her first deliverance from death and the bonus of ten more happy years, these misguided people were still hovering around the corpse to claim another victim. I wanted to cry out to them, "Get off this good man's back and let him live with the memory of a living presence. Let him live with the memory of a courageous, precious lady who blessed all who knew her because she knew that whether she lived or died she was the Lord's."[33] The fact that God is for us doesn't preserve us from all physical harm in this world.

At an Alcoholics Anonymous meeting in the Social Hall of the Colquitt United Methodist Church, I heard this from a participant. In Columbus, Georgia an alcoholic named Roy K. said to a recovering alcoholic Judge, who was working with him, "God

---

[33] Romans 14:8

W. Hamp Watson, Jr.

can't possibly forgive me." He was thinking of how he had messed up his family's life through his addiction. "God can't possibly forgive me!"

The judge said to him, "Well you must think you're better than God."

Roy said, "Oh no, I don't think that."

The judge said, "You must, because if you had a son and he was repentant of his wrong doing and was willing to change his life, you'd forgive him, wouldn't you?"

Roy said, "Yes."

The judge said, "Well then you're not better than God and more loving than God. How can you presume that God is not as much for you as you would be for your son?"[34]

When I was District Superintendent of the Valdosta District, I became aware of how the Tyson Memorial Church in Moultrie was built. It was a beautiful, little brick church serving a more modest part of town. The members were building it and contributing their volunteer labor. One man had given heavily to it, but had also lost his arm after an accident with one of the saws. Economic recession came and they ran out of money to complete the church. At a church conference where they were deciding to quit building, this man got up and waved his stump of an arm in the air and said, "We can't quit. I've got too much invested in this church to quit. Let's keep on building!"

When I was living at Eastman, on my way to McRae, I had a flat on my old car. My lug wrench only twisted the corners off the lugs, without removing them, and I was stuck. I flagged and flagged and finally an old broken down heap screeched to a stop. A guy on his way to Texas got out to cheerfully help me. He used profanity every other word as he drove me several miles back to get a lug wrench that would do the job. Then he insisted on changing the tire himself.

[34] Matthew 7:9

W. Hamp Watson, Jr.

I didn't approve of his profanity, but it made me think about an old novel, *Miriam's Schooling,* where a character called Mrs. Joll was unpleasant, unkempt, and quarrelsome. But her redeeming quality was this—"She comes instantly to the help of anyone, stranger or neighbor in their illness or need." [35]

The novelist says of her, "She has done the one thing which, if there ever is to be a judgment day, will put her on the right hand, when all sorts of scientific people, religious people, students of poetry, people with exquisite emotions, will go to the left and be damned everlastingly."

One day after church at Rincon, I met little redheaded Donny Seckinger out on the front steps. This five year-old hit me with a question—"Why can't I see Jesus?"

I didn't know quite what to say at first. I said, "Have you asked your mother?"

He said, "Yes, I asked my mother and she told me to ask you."

I still didn't know quite what to say, but I began this way, "If you could see him here or if you could see him up there, then he couldn't be everywhere."

This answer seemed to satisfy him. I talked to his mother about it and she said that she had tried to explain to Donny why he couldn't see Jesus and she had told him almost the same thing I had told him. She said, "I tried, but it's so hard to get a child to see. It's something we learn as we grow up." Or do we?[36]

When I was at Wesley Monumental, I got word that my boyhood buddy, Billy, had died the first Tuesday of January. He was my childhood chum, best man at my wedding, but since then our paths parted and we'd only seen each other, at most, three or four times. My first memory of him was when they moved back to Baxley when he was five. He turned six thirty days after me as we started the first day of school together. Being brusque and bullyish, the first mistake he made that day was picking on Bobby

---

[35] Matthew 25
[36] John 16:7

W. Hamp Watson, Jr.

Dubberly who was a little kid. But Billy had not yet learned the principle that "the littlest potatoes are the hardest to peel." So Bobby proceeded to thrash him. I couldn't let that happen to my newfound friend, so I plunged into the fray to help Billy. Having learned his lesson, Billy backed off, but Bobby continued and gave me a whipping I'll never forget for meddling where I had no business.

Billy the Bully and I continued our friendship as I would take my life in my hands to get in a car with him going the seventeen miles from Baxley to Hazlehurst in fifteen minutes, during my teen years. I knew then that Billy would never lead your normal, sedate lifestyle. In the years that followed, he went through two early marriages, incessant bouts with alcoholism, but founded a highly successful business that finally ended in bankruptcy. He was never in church, though his Daddy had an end seat on a pew and his Mama sang in the choir all her life. So when word of his death came, I wondered how the family would take it. His dad had died. His Mama was ninety-four, so I called her and found she'd had a slight stroke and couldn't talk well on the phone. But his sister said she was taking it mighty well. You see, Billy, knowing he had a terminal illness, had shielded his mother until the very last. But his mother had been up Monday to see him and sat and held his hand as she watched him die. The sister said she now seemed broken hearted but serene, if you could be both at the same time.

But his sister had a question for me, the man of the cloth. She said, "Hamp, do you suppose Billy was saved?" When she said this, I was so glad that I had already contacted Billy's current wife. She told me how they had had thirteen years of a good, solid marriage. Billy had joined Alcoholics Anonymous, where he went twice a week, religiously. She said he'd been the most sensitive, kind husband to her that she could ever have wanted. He'd gotten his life back together and through his consummate skill at selling, had helped the new owners of his old company get it back on its feet.

I was able to tell his sister that it was my conviction that AA with its Twelve Step Program of recovery was patterned after time-honored principles of our faith—things like:

- "Our lives had become unmanageable and only a power greater than ourselves could restore us to sanity",

W. Hamp Watson, Jr.

- "Turning our lives over to God as we understood God",
- "Admitting to God, to ourselves, and to another human being the exact nature of our wrongs"
- "Making amends to people we had hurt", and
- "Carrying this message to others."

I was able to say to his sister, I'm in sales, not in management in this faith business, and I don't place people into cubbyholes in the afterlife, but that I could trust Billy to a merciful God who had helped keep him sober for thirteen years.

In fact, I think I know what happened that first Tuesday in January. I don't know how, or where, and I can't spell out the furniture or the particulars of it, but I think there was an encounter that went something like this. "Jesus looked at him and said, 'You are Billy the Bully? No! You are to be called William the Conqueror[37]—one who has striven with alcohol and self and God and has prevailed.'"[38]

When I first started out in the ministry, I served among a people who did not have the same views on race that I held. At the time it was a very hot issue; and at a youth meeting following church one night, I gave rather radical expression to some of my ideas. When we were driving home in the car, Day said, "You're going to hear from that meeting." Worse luck you know, these wives are sometimes right.

By the next morning, two or three men of the Church were incensed at me, and by ten o'clock I was called on the carpet in the chief preacher's office. Using all the language permissible to a preacher and some that I wondered about, he proceeded to take me apart. He told me how these men were angry and he didn't have to tell me about his rejection of me. He sent me from there to see the Chairman of the Board.

He was a lawyer, whom I knew as a man who could use his tongue, and I went trembling and knocked gingerly on his office door. I went in and he smiled at me. I was amazed. I expected to

---

[37] Genesis 32:28
[38] John 1:42

W. Hamp Watson, Jr.

be raked over the coals. But the gist of what he said to me was this. "Hamp, you have seen the effect of your error of expression in the life of this church. I think you know the harm you've done. Let that be your only punishment as far as I'm concerned. I personally respect your freedom of opinion as a person and especially as a minister and I would die for your right to preach what you believe."

We shook hands; I mean really shook, for mine was shaking with gratitude. I left the office and ever since that day I've been searching for someone to whom I can show that same kind of grace.[39]

I went down to the funeral of an honest Certified Public Accountant in Bainbridge. He'd done my taxes free since I was his pastor in 1975. I owed him that trip and a lot more besides. On the way back I ate at a little café in Camilla where I sat across the table from a fellow that I discovered was a salesman for an office supply company. I asked him "What are your best sellers these days?"

He said, "Since the Enron and World Com scandals we just can't keep enough paper shredders in stock."

Would you believe that—a bull market on paper shredders?

Some counsel that if trouble piles up and depression comes, just move on to new territory. The answer to every problem is to change your parking place. I was talking to D. E. Turk in the hall at the courthouse in Abbeville, Georgia, about his ill-fated car. He'd been parking it in front of the courthouse and a lawn mower across the street slung a tin can into it. Somebody picking up a school bus tire let it roll down the front steps and into the side of it. Several suggested to Turk that he'd better change his parking place. He said he didn't think it would do him much good. With a car like that he could park it on a desert island and a trailer truck would run into it.

---

[39] I Peter 4:10

W. Hamp Watson, Jr.

On my first country circuit, I was talking to two men where they were tearing down an old stable fence at a leisurely pace. They were moving slowly. You really had to kind of line your eye up along your finger to tell whether they were moving or not. One of them said, "I saw a feller in such a hurry the other day that he just ran across the yard to pick up a bucket to go slop the hogs."

The other one said, "If you ever see me or Robert in a hurry, you can know that a fish is about to pull a pole in the water."

More of us might live longer with that sort of spirit about things.[40]

I found some pictures for our new family room. I asked the clerk if I could carry them out to the car to let my wife see them, before I made the purchase. I offered to leave more than enough money to cover it with the cashier while I ran right out and right back. She waved the money aside and said, "Go on out. It'll be all right."

The floor manager heard her. He stepped up and said, "Can't do that, Elaine. If he wants to take it out, let him pay for it. Then if he isn't satisfied, you can refund his money."

Then I made my big mistake. I called him over to the side and said, "I know it's none of my business, but wouldn't it have been better to call her aside and tell her about it later and not embarrass her in front of a customer, and I might add, embarrass your customer as well."

He looked me in the eye. He said, "You're right. It **is** none of your business. **I'm** in charge of this department."

So he was. And from the fire that flashed in his eyes, I knew who was in charge of him. He was the type that was so griped by criticism he could never grow by it. [41]

In contrast, Thomas H. Johnson, Sr. told me about two members of his church that were friends, who were going

---

[40] Acts 1:4
[41] Proverbs 1:7, 12:15

W. Hamp Watson, Jr.

on at each other while shopping in a supermarket. One was criticizing the other for the money she was wasting on a highly advertised product, and the other one was casting aspersions on some of the purchases she had made. They were laughing as they laid each other low. At the register, the clerk stopped them and said, "Are you ladies sisters?"

They said, "No."

She said, "Well, I just wondered. You talk to each other like you're sisters."

If we're sons and daughters of God and brothers and sisters in Christ, we ought to be able to offer constructive criticisms to each other without falling out about it. This is one way we can grow, and when we stop growing, we're just walking around to save funeral expenses.

One of my tennis playing, medical doctor friends in a past pastorate was the kind who would repair his own brakes on his Cadillac to save money. But then, he drove the car into the garage to park it, applied the brakes to stop it, and drove right out through the end of the garage. His wife had tried to no avail to keep him from doing it, but after this, she said, "If my husband wants to repair the brakes, I'm sure not going to stand in his way."

I remember going back to my hometown ten years after I graduated from High School and running into an old buddy at the drug store. He was unshaven, unkempt, and looked like he was suffering from a hangover. But he was proudly wearing a jacket, which wasn't quite able to cover his protruding frame. In big, bold letters across the front it said, "Basketball Champs 1947!" Here was a young man confined by a past success he couldn't forget, still stumbling around through life taking odd jobs, and even failing to keep his commitments to his family.

I don't know how it happened, but I remember how pleased I was a couple of years later to see him show up clean-shaven and neat at a Beginning Minister's Workshop I was helping to teach at the Georgia Methodist Pastor's School at Wesleyan College in

W. Hamp Watson, Jr.

Macon. He had somehow been able to forget one of those things which was behind, that supreme success that had made him satisfied with where he was in life, and he was now obviously reaching for the righteousness from God.[42]

During a pastorate where I was struggling to get my people to see that there was a relationship between the run-down nature of all their facilities, and their failure to keep their covenants with God, I wandered one day back to my old home church at Baxley. I went in the church and walked through it. Passing a pew, I thought of many people who were there when I was a boy, that have now gone on. I could see and hear those people who were no longer there in the flesh.

There was Ira Leggett, Postmaster, and Veteran of the Spanish American War. They needed a new parsonage when times were hard and many were opposed to it. But Mr. Ira got up, interrupting the preacher's announcements, just speaking from where he stood at his pew. He said, "You know, I was at the parsonage the other night, and I want to commend this congregation for having one of the most unusual parsonages in the Conference. On that visit, I learned that our preacher is becoming quite an accomplished astronomer. He can just lie in bed at night and study the stars through the holes in the roof." It wasn't long before something was done about the parsonage.

Some people can never be satisfied even when things are going their way. Mr. William Fawley, at prayer Meeting at Bainbridge, told us about the little boy and his father who were dividing up the pie when there were only two pieces left—a little piece and a big piece. The father let the little boy divide the pieces; the little boy took the big piece of pie for himself and gave the little piece of pie to his daddy. His daddy said, "Son, If I had been dividing the pie, I would have given you the big piece, and I would have taken the little piece."

---

[42] Philippians 3:12-14

W. Hamp Watson, Jr.

Little boy said, "Well, what you fussing about, Daddy? You got the little piece, didn't you?"

Ella Lewis died when I was pastor at Wesley Monumental in Savannah. She was the black maid and cook, who saved our lives when we had three little stair-step children at Rincon, Georgia, thirty-five years before her death. I had intended to go out to see her just to express our appreciation. It wouldn't have taken long since Rincon is so close to Savannah. Her daughter let me know when she was brought to Candler Hospital in Savannah and I did get to call on her in the hospital room when she was in a coma.

Later I attended her funeral and was honored when they asked me to get up and say a few words. I don't remember what I said, but the black women who served as flower carriers brought in the wreaths and placed them and as they were doing that, the choir sang a song that I'd never heard before. The theme that kept being expressed in the words was, "Bring me flowers while I can still smell them." I wished that I had.[43]

When we were at Park Avenue United Methodist Church in Valdosta, Jim Perry and about two hundred and fifty of the members put on a Passion Play called, *"God Hath Provided the Lamb."* One time they put it on, two men climbed the hastily made ladders and put the linen cloth under his arms, then took the mallet and loosened the nails, and then gently brought his body down. Then, they laid it down and Joseph started winding the body in the linen cloth and Nicodemus, standing close by, started putting in the herbs and spices as each round was made. Then, Joseph and Nicodemus together carry his body to the tomb. They came up the aisle by us, and I looked at Day… and through my tears, I saw that she had melted in the pew.[44]

In the category of "Of all sad words of tongue or pen" we have the incident at Eastman following the Cub Scout

---

[43] John 19:38-42
[44] John 19:38-42

W. Hamp Watson, Jr.

competition, in which fathers and their sons built little airplanes. They were powered by wound up rubber bands that, when released, would shoot the little aircraft down a wire. Olin Pound and his son, Crawford, had an airplane entered in the race.

Not to be left out, Crawford's younger brother, Dillard, had also built a plane with his Dad's help. He was not old enough to be a Cub Scout, but the officials let him race his plane for fun. Dillard's airplane was released, but somehow, the rubber band broke and the plane just fizzled and came to a quick stop on the wire, while other aircraft sped to victory.

In the car on the way home, Dillard sought to comfort his father. He said, "Daddy, mine woulda won if it woulda went!"

In the category of putting the responsibility where it belongs, at Eastman, Jean Pound taught in the Dodge County Elementary Schools. She gave a spelling test, graded the papers quickly, and handed out the grades. When she got her paper, one of her students sashayed up to Jean's desk and said, "A zero! A zero! Mrs. Pound, you ain't learned us nothing!"

Martin Luther in *Table Talk,* said, "Birds lack faith; they fly away when you mean them no harm." I didn't discover fully what he meant until one summer morning I was going over to my study, and a lovely brown thrasher had become trapped in the social hall of the Rincon Methodist Church. As I came in the door, he got frightened and began to flutter and beat the panes of glass with his wings, terrified by my presence. He was trying to get out of the room. I could have left, but I wanted to release this bird and let it out. But you know how they do .He flew right up into the top of the building.

Then finally, I thought I saw my chance to let him go free. As he got over against a certain window, I went over and grabbed the window quickly and pulled it down. As I pulled down the top half of the window, the fear-crazed bird fluttered right into the crack and as I pulled the window down, I felt the crunch. His neck was broken. He fluttered once or twice and fell to the floor. I carried

W. Hamp Watson, Jr.

him outside and tried to lift him up to fly,but I saw that his life was gone.[45]

Do people lack faith?

Have you ever noted how often we will say to others, "I don't care what people think!" when we really do very much care what people think? In fact the times we say, "I don't care what people think!" it's usually when we're in a group of people or with persons who admire those who say, "I don't care what people think."

In the days that I was the Pastor of Park Avenue United Methodist Church in Valdosta, I was into jogging for my health in the neighborhood in the early mornings. One Sunday morning, I had started out from the parsonage on my usual jog. Our parsonage was on Slater Street, directly behind the church and facing the property of Northside Baptist Church. As I left our yard, I noted that during the night Saturday night, someone had been generous enough to contribute a large number of beer cans that littered the front lawn of the parsonage and the lawn between the parsonage and the Park Avenue Church. That wouldn't do. What would our members think as they arrived for Sunday School and Church and saw all these beer cans on their pastor's lawn?

Very quickly I stopped my jog and gathered up all the beer cans and was just before putting them in the trash can that was behind our parsonage. At that moment, I thought, "What will the City Sanitation workers think when they come to empty the trash and find all these beer cans in the Methodist Preacher's garbage?"

So very quickly, I reversed my steps, and went across the street and threw them into the large dumpster behind the Northside Baptist Church. As I put the last beer can in, I thought to myself, "And I'm the guy that doesn't care what people think!"[46]

At Wesley Monumental, on a visit to her home, I came to understand a little better why this member of mine had

---

[45] John 8:36
[46] Matthew 6:1

such an impact for righteousness. She constantly fought for the preservation of God's creation. She was a gregarious, ecologically activistic philanthropist. Where did she come up with such boundless energy for good? On that visit, while she was preparing refreshments for my wife and me, I found the answer on her refrigerator door. Some words were held on to the door by a magnet that said, "Dull Women Have Clean Houses."

Beneath the picture of a spray of beautiful yellow flowers this was the caption; these were the words:

Help me to feel in the rush of the passing,
The stillness of the eternal.

You see, as busy as she was and always is, she had been listening to the sound of silence.[47]

Quinton Shearouse was a twenty-one year old clean cut crew cut in our Bethesda Church in Effingham County. He drove thirty miles every Sunday to work with our youth group. He had his first job and was tithing, giving forty dollars a week to the church in 1958. At his grandfather's house on Thanksgiving day he made the mistake of getting on one of these little go-carts to ride it in the yard. It was the first time he'd ever been on one. He got the accelerator confused with the brake and shot out of the yard right in front of a semi on Georgia Highway 17. He was killed instantly—didn't know what hit him.

After the funeral, about a month later, the treasurer of the church told me that Quinton's daddy, Earl Shearouse, had doubled his pledge and giving to the church. I thought at first when I heard this, that his motive must have been a sense of responsibility as a family unit to make up for the loss of that much income to the church. But time showed me otherwise. In the years that followed, whenever any other cause came up, Earl and Lorene, his mother and father, would give and give heavily. They made gifts to Kingdom Builder's Club, Epworth by the Sea, Magnolia Manor, The Methodist Children's Home—you name it.

---

[47] I Kings 19:12

W. Hamp Watson, Jr.

As I talked to Earl, I discovered that he gave because he enjoyed giving. Now I understand why he doubled his pledge after Quinton's death. In a time of great sorrow, he turned even more to a practice that had never failed to bring him great joy.[48]

On a Wednesday night at Dooly Camp Ground, we were in the middle of the service. There were sixty young people present in the service with about half of them singing from the choir loft. A storm came up and the thunder rolled. The lights went out under that old tabernacle. We kept singing with the lights out, singing from hymn to hymn. We were singing medleys from memory because we couldn't see. When the time for the preaching came, people went out and turned on lights in the cars. The thunder was still rolling and big-voiced Joe Bridges, whose voice sounded like the thunder that kept beating a steady accompaniment, preached.

When the service ended, there were sixty youth crying at the altar. We were up until midnight singing and praising God, and those youth were talking to the counselors.

It was interesting to hear the different accounts of that night after it was over. From a nearby city, some folks, who had dropped into the service for only that evening had a good description of it to share the next day. For them, it explained what happened very well. They said, "They had a thunderstorm over at Dooly; and the lights went out. The young people were so scared; and it was all so eerie that when the preacher played on their emotions, they started coming to the altar and crying." It was purely an emotional reaction provoked by a thunderstorm. The casual, disinterested camp-meeting attendee that night stood by and said that it had thundered.[49]

But that wasn't the whole account. Four young people, that year, thought it was the voice of God calling them to preach. Five young people thought it was the voice of God calling them to church-related vocations. Thirty or forty thought it was the voice of God calling them to rededicate their lives; and there has been

---

[48] II Corinthians 8:3, 9:7
[49] John 12:27-29

W. Hamp Watson, Jr.

such a spiritual carry-over from year to year since that time, that thirty young people have entered the ministry from that place.

Back when "Speaking in Tongues" had been adopted by some elements in the church as mandatory and the only clear sign that a person was truly "baptized by the Holy Spirit," several of us Savannah pastors were meeting with a psychiatrist in Savannah. We would bring to him knotty problems we were having in counseling and he would offer his insights to help us. He told us one day about a young patient that came to him.

His mother brought this eleven-year-old in because he was doing poorly in school and had all sorts of psychological problems. It was early in this psychiatrist's practice, so he just started where you and I would. He said to this little boy, "What's the matter, Son?"

This touched off a veritable explosion of language, rapid-fire but clearly understandable. The little boy said, "Doctor, things jes' ain't been right since my Daddy died. I's in 'dis school and doing good in 'dis school, but when my Daddy died, my Mama took me out of 'dat school and put me in 'nother school. She made me go to church wid' her. I been go church wid' my Daddy, but she made me go to church wid' her where 'dey tell me I going to Hell.

'Dey tell me I going to Hell if I play marbles. 'Dey tell me I going to Hell if I watch telebision. 'Dey tell me I going to Hell if I don't speak in tongues.

Well now, I stopped playing marbles. I quit watching telebision. But I can't speak in no tongues! I tries and I tries. I get down on my knees at night and I pray to 'de Lord to help me speak in tongues; but I still can't talk nothin' but Geechee!"

Doesn't your heart go out to that little boy; and doesn't it go out to anyone who gets caught in the trap of believing that any **one** of God's gifts of the Spirit is mandatory, unless it be love?[50]

To end these *Pearls,* let me tell you about Fred and Lily. They had five children and lived in a house much too

---

[50] I Corinthians 12:28-30, 13:1

W. Hamp Watson, Jr.

small in the old part of town. At a local plant, he was shop foreman who kept all the machines running and invented many of them. They had three of those children in college. But I discovered, quite by accident, that Fred and Lily were perhaps the largest contributors to our church, if you measured it as percentage of their income. The multimillionaire church member who owned the plant was also quite generous, but couldn't approach their percentage.

Lily was always out visiting the sick and the shut-ins. She let the house go more than she should, but she found with her overflowing heart of love that there was just not enough time in the day to do all that she was interested in doing for others and her family.

After we left there, we got word that Lily had developed ALS—Amyotropic Lateral Sclerosis (Lou Gherig's Disease), which brings about gradual deterioration always ending in death, and she knew it. That's why the front of the bulletin from my old church, which I received at the peak of the onslaught of her disease, is one that I've kept across the years. It had Lily's latest rhyme on it. It proved to be her last offering. Here it is:

> Now! Now! Now!
> You only have the now!
> The now to do the master's will,
> The now to listen and be still.
> Now! Now! Now!
> The clock of life repeats.
> Now is the time to turn to Him,
> Love Him enough to learn from Him.
> Now! Now! Now!
> Tomorrow may be too late.
> Let Jesus have your full control,
> And then you will be fully whole.
> Now! Now! Now!
> "The hour is late!" we hear him say.
> The only time you have is now.
> O, won't you listen and obey![51]

---

[51] I Thessalonians 3:8

W. Hamp Watson, Jr.

Index

Chestnuts from the Family Tree

In my wife's brother's family there was a little girl named Hattie Howard. When we all sat at Mrs. Wilson's table for a meal one day, Hattie Howard kept putting her knees up to the table. She was warned about it two or three times, but persisted. Finally, her mother said, "I wish that bad little girl that keeps putting her knees up to the table would go away and my good Hattie Howard would come back."

That caught her attention, and she said, "Mama, can I tell God anything I want to?"

Her mother said, "Of course, Hattie."

Immediately, Hattie Howard went over and knelt down at the window at the end of the dining room in full sight of the whole family. They all were quiet as she finished her prayer. Then she returned to her place at the table and said, "Mama, do you know what I told God?"

Her mother said, "No, Darling, what?"

Hattie Howard said, "I told God to kill that bad little girl!"

In the shocked silence, her mother finally recovered to say, "Hattie Howard, maybe you should have just asked God to make that bad little girl better."

Hattie Howard got up and headed back to her place of prayer at the window ledge. She said, "OK, she ain't kilt yet; I'll go back and tell him."[1]

I remember when they discovered I needed glasses in grammar school. The teacher began to be suspicious because she noticed that when a test was put on the blackboard, I would get down on the floor and crawl up close to read the questions. If I walked upright to the board to read them, the class would scream at me for blocking their vision, so I just crawled. The Kiwanis Club was buying glasses for poor children and so they adopted me as a project. I remember going up to Calhoun's Drug

---

[1] Matthew 7:7

W. Hamp Watson, Jr.

Store when Dr. L. N. Huff from Atlanta was holding forth. He sat me in a chair and said, "Read those letters on the screen."

I said, "What letters?" All I could see was a blank, blurry screen. Then he started flipping different lenses in front of my face until a vision appeared to me that I never had seen before. Those letters he had been talking about stood out in bold, black type. He put the glasses on me that very day, and I left the drugstore running home, seeing the whole, big, beautiful world in a glorious detail that I never had seen before. There are few times in my life that I can remember being as happy as I was then, unless it was at Dooly Camp Ground, during a great worship week, when for the first time I saw all my companions there through the eye of God.[2]

After our retirement to Macon, our children were after us to get a "Power of Attorney, Living Will, and Power of Health Care Attorney" series of papers drawn up by a lawyer. We resolved to contact Warren Plowden, South Georgia Conference Chancellor, to do the job for us. His office was in a bank building on Cherry Street. I scouted it out in advance and thought that I would have to take Day in a wheelchair because there was a steep step right off the street to access the elevator. I learned later that if we had gone in the front of the bank there would have been no problem.

We made it up the elevator to his office, signed the papers and were on our way out. I was backing through the glass door pulling Day in the chair. I had forgotten that step. Down we went. I dumped Day out on my way down.

I said, "Honey, our children are going to get to use those papers today!"

As it happened, thank God, neither of us was seriously hurt.

When I was about nine years old, my father, the County Attorney in Baxley, Georgia, came down with a depressive psychosis. We kept him at home until my mother died when I was sixteen, and we had to have him committed to the

---

[2] II Corinthians 5:16

W. Hamp Watson, Jr.

State Mental Hospital where he died two years later. So all the Watson children worked to help make ends meet. Selling newspapers on the street corners and in hotels of Baxley, I'd yell out, "Paper, paper, read all about it!" We never had any "Extras" to shout out at Baxley. But in that process, I came into contact with two phrases that have haunted my life. I overheard two old codgers on the street corner. One said, "Who is that boy yelling his head off?"

The other one said, "Why that's Wade Watson's boy." That was the first phrase—"Wade Watson's boy."

The second phrase came from the first man. He said, "You know, he was a fine man."

I knew Daddy had taught the Men's Bible Class for fifteen years before he got sick. I remembered that he sang bass in the choir. I remembered those winter Sunday nights at church when I'd go to sleep on the front pew and wake up in my father's arms. But, "Wade Watson's boy—You know, he was a fine man." I began to feel that maybe I ought to at least try to live like the son of a fine man.

Do you have any phrases that haunt your life?

I know a great lady who laughs at life and the time to come. She's a pistol ball. Her mother died at forty-eight, and so at twenty years of age she was left with responsibility for finishing raising a younger brother and caring for a mentally ill father and sister. In mid-life, she lost her husband one month and the next month underwent a modified radical mastectomy. Instead of withdrawing from life, within a year she went skiing for the first time in her life in Aspen, Colorado.

She pitched six years for her women's softball team and got on stage and clogged with her less than slim body for a community benefit. To a brother-in-law, who had to have a piece of his ear cut off to prevent the spread of cancer, she said, "We'll be all right won't we, Royce, as long as we have enough parts left to be cut off?"

She works in the church, sings in the choir, once lead a children's choir, and was treasurer for the building fund for the

W. Hamp Watson, Jr.

new social hall. She bought a house adjoining the church property because she was afraid the price might dim the trustees' vision to buy it, and she deeded it to the church. It's in use now by the church.

But until recently, she was never asked to say anything about her giving to the church. She was quite reluctant at first, but finally agreed. So for her stewardship witness to the church, she said, "My mother died of cancer, but I still had my church. My father was mentally ill for ten years before his death, but all during his illness and after his death, I still had my church. I lost Raymond and buried him from the church, but I still had my church. My children left home for marriage or work and the nest was empty, but guess what! I still had my church. I thank God for my church, and I'm going to support it with all I can now and with some of what I leave after I'm gone." Gratitude![3]

My wife's mother, "Ma," Mrs. F. H. Wilson of Griffin, Georgia, loved to tell about the little boy in the neighborhood who was a strange little fellow. He would leave his house and come try to play down at the Wilson's with the children there. But he didn't know how to play. He'd be as ornery as he knew how to be. He'd call the girls names. He'd say, "You old elephlunt mule!" He was trying to call them an elephant mule. "Ma" tried to give him refreshments or interest him in a storybook, but always he shied away and rejected any attention. But one afternoon she was lying down on her bed, reading a magazine preparatory to her nap, when she noticed he had come in the house. He came in her room and finally ventured up to the bed. As she turned the pages and commented on the pictures in the magazine, he leaned closer and got up on the bed beside her. She was afraid to breathe for fear she would frighten him away and break the spell.

His body touched hers as he looked at the pictures, and then in an unguarded moment, he leaned over and kissed her on the cheek. As if he couldn't believe what he'd done, he drew back and said to "Ma," "Don't you do that again!"

---

[3] I Peter 2:21

W. Hamp Watson, Jr.

How "Ma" would laugh when she told that, because she knew that he was just exhibiting the fact that there's a secret down inside everyone of us that's trying for all its worth to come out.[4]

Let's call him Jones. That's not his name, but he was a real man who lived not far from here. It happens that he was an elder in the Presbyterian Church, though he could just as well have been a deacon in the Baptist or a Board Member in the Methodist. He prayed publicly at church. He was an avid defender of the true faith as he saw it, and he was quick to spot a heresy. He was so devoted that he would go down to the city jail on Sunday afternoon to talk to the prisoners about Christ and have prayer.

Jones had a good income, but he wouldn't put out one red cent to get his daughter through college or to pay her wedding expenses. His wife taught school in order to provide these things. She scrimped and saved in order to provide the bare necessities for living. Before he died with everything he owned in the bank, my Father-in-law said, "If he were to have to move, all he'd have to do would be to put out the fire and call the dog he's so tight." When his aged mother, who lived several blocks down the street, was sick, his wife prepared her meals and carried them to her. Jones would walk up to her house fifteen minutes ahead of mealtime and sit on the porch and watch his frail wife stumbling under the heavy tray with his and his mother's supper on it. He wouldn't think of waiting to carry the tray himself.

My Father-in-law had another apt phrase. He said, "If you knew his home life and you were out shooting Christians, you wouldn't cock your gun at him."[5]

My Brother-in-law, Ben, didn't know he was teaching anything when he sat watching the TV one night. Ben was feeling pretty good because he had stayed home baby sitting with their two small boys while his wife went to a night circle meeting at the church. So it shocked him when four-year-old Scott

---

[4] Colossians 3:3-4
[5] Ephesians 5:25

W. Hamp Watson, Jr.

came up, leaned against his knee and said, "Daddy, mens don't go to church much, do they?" You see, you're elected Dad, whether or not you run.[6]

When I was little, one morning when I got up and went into the kitchen, my grandmama said to me, "Wade Hampton, did you wash your face?"

I said, "No, Grandmama."

She said, "Did you comb your hair?"

I had some then, and I said, "No Grandmama."

She said, "Did you brush your teeth?"

I said, "No, Grandmama."

She said, "Well, go back and do it."

The next morning when I smelled the bacon frying, I got up and went into the kitchen. My grandmama said to me, "Wade Hampton, did you wash your face?"

I said, "No, Grandmama."

She said, "Did you comb your hair?"

I said, "No Grandmama."

She said, "Did you brush your teeth?"

I said, "No, Grandmama."

She said, "Well, go back and do it."

Every morning she'd make me so mad when I would go into the kitchen; she'd say, "Wade Hampton," (She always called me Wade Hampton when she was serious about anything.) "Wade Hampton, did you wash your face, comb your hair, brush your teeth?"

And I'd say, "No, Grandmama."

And she'd say, "Well, go back and do it."

I became a twelve-year-old seventh grader and I fell madly in love with a little yellow-headed girl named Nell Briscoe. And you know, the very next morning when I got up and went into the kitchen, my grandmama didn't have to say a word. Before she opened her mouth, I threw my bright and shining freshly washed face up toward her; I flashed my big old Ipana smile at her; and I gave one more twist of the comb to my hair that was slicked down

---

[6] Proverbs 22:6

W. Hamp Watson, Jr.

like it had molasses on it. With my love for Nell, Grandmama's outward demand had become my inward desire; and I was free from her nagging demands.[7]

My daughter, who had bi-lateral mastectomies herself, has fitted people for prostheses as an adjunct service of the hospital down in Albany. She's told us that a patient who's gone through this will come in to be fitted, and be morose, unresponsive, depressed and short with her as she tries to help them. But the minute they discover that she's gone through their same problem, it's as though the sunlight breaks through the dark night of their gloom. They become cooperative and responsive and grateful for what she's trying to do for them. People in my pastorates who have lost children have told me that the most help they got in their struggle to come back to life was from other bereaved parents. Like cures like. The antidote for snakebite is made from the snake's venom. The serpent heals the serpent's sting.[8]

Day's sister, Jane, had a friend in Macon who had a little girl. So, when she was expecting again, she asked God for a "real boy." After the boy came, he proved to be a real stem-winder. Jane's son, Scott, referred to him always as "My mad friend," because he was always angry and into something. So the mother laughed and said to Jane one day, "You better be careful what you ask for because you're liable to get it."[9]

Day's first cousin, Kebie, though a Methodist, went to Bessie Tift Baptist College at Forsyth, Georgia, back in the dark ages when Methodists and Baptists argued about such inconsequential things as to whether once you're saved, you're always saved. It was eternal security for the Baptists as opposed to

---

[7] Galatians 2:15-21
[8] John 3:14
[9] I Kings 3:5-12

W. Hamp Watson, Jr.

free will and falling from grace for the Methodists. Since Kebie had grown up in a good Methodist home, where we not only believed in "falling from grace" but also regularly practiced it, she got into an argument with one of her Baptist professors about this doctrine. He said, "Miss Scott, you were born a Scott, you are now a Scott, and you will always be a Scott."

Kebie rolled those Southern eyes and said "I shuwah do hope not!" And the class disintegrated.

We can fall from grace, or we can find "Amazing Grace." We don't have to stay the way we are. We can change our names.[10]

I used to tell a story to my children about a little boy who got up on the wrong side of the bed one morning. The very first thing he did to show his displeasure at the world was to take the toothpaste and squeeze it out all around the edge of the lavatory. Not content with that he went on down the street on the way to school and saw Mrs. Brown's apple tree. He climbed over the fence, climbed the tree, and shook all the apples off the tree. Not content with that he went on down the street and passed the barbershop. He saw a man in there lying down to get a shave, with his face all covered with a cloth while the barber had to go into the back of the shop for just a moment. So he ran in quickly, took the scissors and cut all the man's hair off and ran out of the barbershop.

Of course, by the time the little boy got home from school that afternoon, his mother had the message about what he'd done and she met him at the door. She said, "Johnny, I've heard about the terrible things you've done today, and if you don't go back and undo every bad thing that you've done today, I'm going to whip you within an inch of your life."

This scared him so much that he ran back into the bathroom and gathered up all the toothpaste and put it back in the tube. He left there and ran on down the street and climbed over the fence and grabbed the apples and put them back on the tree and they began to grow. He left there and ran back down the street to the barbershop. There was the man still lying in the chair. He picked

---

[10] John 1:42

W. Hamp Watson, Jr.

the hair up off the floor, put it back on the man's head and it started to grow. Then he ran back home, smiled at his mother and said, "Mother, I have undone everything that I did wrong today."

She said, "That's fine, Johnny. You're forgiven."

Then I would say to my children, "What's wrong with that story?"

My youngest said to me, "Daddy, you can't put toothpaste back in a tube."

That's right. And you can't put apples back on a tree and expect them to grow. And I'm living testimony that you can't put hair back on a man's head.

Some things are better never done in the first place.[11]

Once, when two of our grandsons were visiting, the younger one got on the Internet with my computer and played some games, but soon tired of that. Then it was off to the amusement park, Starcadia. He didn't want to play miniature golf with his Dad and brother. That was "boring," so I bought him enough tokens to play about every game in the place and even ride a real little racecar around the track. He spotted that high wall they have outside where you put on a harness and test your skill climbing it until you can ring a bell at the top. I saw him almost smile after he had accomplished that twice. But you know what really did the trick?

When we got out of the place, already late to come home to supper, their car had a flat tire. His Dad started to change it, but had real difficulty bending over and turning that lug wrench on the jack that was so long it kept hitting the ground and wouldn't turn much—a really laborious little job. Come to find out that this boy had been with his mother when she had a flat and had helped her change it. He got down there on the ground, took that lug wrench and jack and lifted that car, so his Dad could get the tire off. He was small enough and low-down enough to work in that tight little space. We came in a little late to supper, but with a happy Jordan, who poured out the story of our adventures to the waiting women.

---

[11] John 19:14

W. Hamp Watson, Jr.

When he was just a little tyke in his other grandfather's arms, the older of these two grandsons received what should have been a compliment from a gushing lady. She said, "Oh what a beautiful baby!"

The little tyke turned in Jimmy Bentley's arms to face the lady and said, "Hamp's not a baby! Hamp's a boy!"

All of us must arrive on the human stage with some need to protect our self-image. Many of us want to escape childhood nicknames that seem to indicate less than mature, adult powers of decision and autonomy. Though I loved growing up in Baxley, Georgia, one of the consolations in leaving there was escaping the name "Hampy." I know of at least two maturing young people in my last large congregation—one from an affluent home, and one from a background of deprivation and poverty—who during my pastorate there consciously shifted the names they were originally called by their parents to the second name given them. I had a suspicion that it had something to do with their asserting for themselves a new, autonomous image of who they were and who they wanted to become as persons in their own right. Indeed, "Hamp's not a baby! Hamp's a boy!"

I remember growing up in Baxley, Georgia in pre-Civil Rights days. It was common for somebody turning twenty-one to say, "I'm free, white, and twenty-one!"[12] They were asserting their man-hood and they thought their freedom. But it was the kind of freedom that gave them license to oppress and sometimes, like out in Mississippi, even feel righteous like Mr. Edgar Killen who was recently convicted by a jury for masterminding the killing of those three Civil Rights workers back in the sixties. I remember the horror I felt as a child when a black man was chased by a mob that hit him repeatedly with a pulpwood hook, as he tried to scramble out of the hedge in front of my house. He had presumably been sassy to a white woman up at the Barnes Hotel.

---

[12] Galatians 5:1-14

W. Hamp Watson, Jr.

I remember when, shortly after I had joined the church at Baxley, Georgia, as a little boy, I took my nickel to Sunday School. But when the plate passed that morning I just made a motion at the plate and kept my nickel. That afternoon I got an ice cream cone with that nickel. But strangely, that ice cream tasted like paste. It stuck in my throat. I couldn't sing the songs that night at church and when pastor J. Lytle Jones greeted me, I averted my eyes, as I gave him a limp fish for a hand. Not until I told my mother what I had done, took my grounding, and doubled the gift the next Sunday, did I get back the joy of going to class with my buddies. I was also able to pray again, "Now I lay me down to sleep," and go to sleep without tossing and turning.[13]

The preacher's son was J. Lytle Jones, Jr. He was two years older than I was and was the newly elected President of the Secret Club. So far there was only one other member of the club, Melville Wood, who lived down Anthony Street and was nine years old. I looked up to these older men. I practically worshipped them from my measly seven years. I lived for what gems of wisdom they might drop my way and for what activities they might let me engage in with them. I was under consideration for membership in the Secret Club, and I saw them coming down the sidewalk, just out of their secret meeting. I waited, fidgety with excitement, until they could get close enough to tell me that I was going to be allowed to join.

But when they got near me, they were both silent and secretive. J. Lytle, the President, handed me what looked like a piece of chewing gum. They went on down the street and left me with it. It wasn't gum at all. It was a little note folded to look like chewing gum wrapped up in a Juicy Fruit wrapper. I opened the paper with trembling fingers, got the tin foil that it used to come in loose, and I read the message I found inside. It said, "You can't be a member of our club." I ran to my backyard, holed up in my little tent, and cried most of the rest of the afternoon.[14]

---

[13] Psalm 32:3-5
[14] James 2:1-9

W. Hamp Watson, Jr.

A dear, old childless couple, Dr. & Mrs. Comer Woodward of Emory, lived to be in their eighties together. When I was in their home one day, Aunt Mary had been chiding Uncle Comer about something, and he had said, "Mary, do you love me?"

She said, "Comer, you know I love you from the top of your head to the bottom of your toes."

Uncle Comer's white head turned and his eyes twinkled and he said, "Well, Mary, let's live like it then!"[15]

When I was eight or nine years old, my cousin, Dennis, from the big city of Philadelphia, came to visit me in Baxley, Georgia, and I was showing him around town, roaming as little boys will do. We came to one of my favorite places, a blacksmith shop, where the smithy would take the red-hot horseshoe from the bellows and bang it into shape on the heavy anvil before it cooled and hardened. The smell of the hot metal mingled with the odor of the horses waiting to be shod. In those days, we had two big livery stables in Baxley where mules were kept and sold for farming and horses were used for pleasure by a number of families in town. When my older cousin saw that bellows and anvil and mallet—the whole operation of the blacksmith shop—he said, "Boy, is that thing ever out of date!"

I didn't know then how right he was, for by the time I reached high school, the livery stables were gone and the blacksmith shop was gone, replaced by the tractor and the automobile; and the smell of the animals no longer wafted its way over the town.

O ur daughter, Susan, loves to tell about the yard sale in Albany, Georgia, where a little boy about seven or so found a typewriter and was so proud when he talked his parents into buying it for him. He said, "I have heard of these." We look now at an old adding machine, a marvel in its time, and say, "Boy is that thing ever out of date!"

Think about Ruth in the Old Testament, this foreigner, Moabite, Gentile woman who became the great-great-great-great

---

[15] John 21:15-17

W. Hamp Watson, Jr.

grandmother of Jesus Christ. Look at this widowed Ruth, who was so loyal to her mother-in-law that she threw off her pleas to go back to her homeland where she could be safe and cared for. She said, "Entreat me not to leave thee, nor to seek from following after thee, for whither thou goest I will go and where thou lodgest I will lodge. Thy people shall be my people and thy God my God.[16]

This Ruth used a sickle to gather the wheat left in the field for the poor. Now we've improved upon Ruth's sickle. If she came back today, we'd put her sickle in a museum. We have machines that storm across the fields and harvest more in an hour than Ruth, with her sickle, could harvest in a lifetime. We've improved upon Ruth's sickle, but have we improved upon Ruth—upon her loyalty and love? I don't think so. There won't be a time in human history when children and youth and adults don't need to be reminded of what Ruth did and what that means for our life today. There are some things that never grow out-of-date.[17]

"Ma," my mother-in-law, told me before she died about being in a new antique shop out of Greensboro, North Carolina, with her niece, Mary Morecock. As you can imagine, these two ladies were having a ball. They were going about from item to item enthusiastically commenting on everything there. It was full of the most beautiful china and old silver and cut glass. "Ma" would say to Mary, "And here is a tea pitcher."

Mary would say to Ma, "Here's a fantastic old sugar bowl." And so they went on in avid conversation naming off item after item.

"And here's a gravy boat."

"And here's a cake keeper."

Suddenly through all their chatter they heard a little voice say, "And here's a little girl!"

They looked down and saw a little girl, with pencil and pad, drawing pictures. She was a child of the neighborhood who was accustomed to being in the shop every day, who was afraid she was

---

[16] Ruth 1:16
[17] Matthew 5:17-20

W. Hamp Watson, Jr.

not going to be noticed by these ladies, who were so overwhelmed by the glamorous offerings of the shop.

S liding Rock, North Carolina, which is between Brevard and the Blue Ridge Parkway, is about one hundred and fifty feet of slick as glass rock with water coursing over it from a natural stream that drops gradually and then precipitously about thirty feet into an icy, exhilarating pool below. I saw it with Day several years ago but didn't have my swimsuit or tennis shoes with me and had to watch all the children and youth and some brave adults sliding down sliding rock. So this time, I got my son and his wife and one daughter, and while Day watched and worried, we all slid down sliding rock. I thought, two hundred and fifty million years before Jim and Tammy Baker came up with the water slide at Heritage Village USA, in South Carolina, the Lord put sliding rock in North Carolina for our pleasure.

But Betty and Wade and Ann and I noticed a strange thing. Every time we climbed back up the rock to slide down again, we would have to fight our way past a line of those standing and blocking the point of entry, who were paralyzed by fear. They had on the attire, they were dressed in swimsuits and tennis shoes, but they were afraid to slide. They were standing between fear and faith and the fun they were being denied.[18]

"Ma," my wife's mother, told me about an interesting little practice she always followed when her daughters were at the dating age. She said, "In those years, I always tried to just make myself available. I'd take a nap in the afternoon so that I could stay up late at night, even if it was until midnight to have a before bedtime snack with any of my girls after they came in off a date. And when we were eating together, they would just bubble over with the events of the evening. They would talk about how so and so looked, about how silly he was. They'd talk about whether something they did was right or wrong. I've got enough sense to know they wouldn't share everything, but they would share with

[18] Matthew 14:22-33

W. Hamp Watson, Jr.

me most of what had gone on, and it was at those times that I had my chance to get my two cents in. If I waited until the next morning, they never would share.

At breakfast I could ask, 'Marie, did you have a nice time on your date last night?'

She'd shrug her shoulders and say, 'It was O.K.' That would be the end of it. So I always made it a practice to stay up with my daughters." I'd say she was a mother who took care to store up the right things so she'd have the right things to give.[19]

It was somewhere in my childhood between six and nine years of age. It was before my father became mentally ill and I was assigned to sleep in the back bedroom with him and be his caretaker. It was before my mother got the breast cancers that killed her at age forty-eight. I began to have risons that covered my body. They'd call them staphylococcus infections today, but they were quite debilitating. I'd have to stay in the house, covered with that old black ichthyol ointment and bandages, and couldn't go outside and play with my buddies. I guess I was whining a little too much one day, and my mother sat me down and said, "Wade Hampton!"

When she was serious about something, she always called me "Wade Hampton." She said, "Wade Hampton, you need to learn two things: First, there is no way you can whine to make anybody around you enjoy hearing it. Second, even if you spend the rest of your life in a wheelchair or bed, it can be a life full of joy."

My wife's mother, "Ma," had a friend with two little girls. She missed some money off her dresser, and that afternoon after school, her oldest daughter came in upset. She said, "Judy bought ice cream at school, but you didn't give me any money for ice cream!"

The mother said, "I didn't give Judy any money."

The daughter said, "Well, she sure bought some."

---

[19] Acts 3:6

W. Hamp Watson, Jr.

When Judy came in, the mother said, "Judy, did you buy some ice cream at school?"

Judy said, "No, M'aam."

Her mother said, "Well, I know you did. And I know that you stole the money to buy it off my dresser this morning. That's true, isn't it?"

Judy said, "Yes, M'aam."

Her mother said, "Now Judy, when you told me you didn't buy any ice cream that was lying. And when you took the money off my dresser without asking my permission, that was stealing."

Judy said, "Well, us all got our little faults, and mine's just lying and stealing."

I'm not clear on the details but "Ma," my wife's mother, had a friend that told her about a flock of geese on a farm. The geese got into some discarded scuppernong hulls that were left in a ditch after the juice was used to make scuppernong wine. The hulls had fermented and the geese got so drunk that they succumbed to the effects and fell into a deep sleep. The hands on the farm discovered them there and, supposing they were dead, plucked all their feathers to make feather beds. They had to salvage something from this terrible loss. They just threw the carcasses back in the ditch to bury later.

Sunday morning, as the family was leaving in the buggy for church, they were greeted by a procession of giddy geese that were stark naked as they waddled up the lane that led to the house.

My son, Wade, who loved to hear "Ma" tell this story, said, "Daddy, I don't know what big idea is in it, but you have to include it."

Since medical doctors were the elite of our town, that was my earliest voiced vocational choice. I just wanted to be one of the richest persons in any town I lived in. But all along the way, strong lay people, and the loving community of the Baxley Methodist Church conspired to lead me in a different direction. After Mother's death, and Dad went to the State Hospital, there

W. Hamp Watson, Jr.

was not a ghost of a chance to go to college. But my pastor, Ab Quillian, put my name in the Wesleyan Christian Advocate as a boy who could lead singing. That summer I got enough honorariums singing in Camp Meetings and Revivals to pay off a seven hundred dollar grocery debt, with enough left over to combine with my sister Lenna's help and a scholarship the preacher's wife got me, to go to Emory Junior College at Valdosta.

While at Valdosta studying pre-med, I got an invitation from G. Ross Freeman and A. W. Reese to come back to Baxley, lead the singing and be teamed with Dr. Harry Denman in a countywide revival in Baxley. When they tried to give Harry a three-hundred-dollar honorarium, he refused. He said, "I don't need it. The Board of Evangelism pays me. Give it to that boy. He says he's going to be a doctor. He's not going to be a doctor. He's going to be a preacher. Give it to him."

S inging led me into most of what's been good in my life. Something was working on me, and I knew it was when I was teamed as song-leader at Dooly Camp Meeting for two straight summers with Frank Robertson and Tom Whiting. I had to live in the preachers' tent with those two giants of the faith, and at the end of the second summer, I had to have some of that. I had to say almost in the words of Ruth, "Entreat me not to leave thee nor to seek from following after thee...Thy people shall be my people and thy God my God."[20]

A s Junior Pastor and Minister of Music at First Methodist Church in Griffin, Georgia, I fell in love with Day Wilson whom I met in the vestibule of the church after I'd preached my first sermon. She married me anyway. I went to her dentist father as a patient when things were getting serious. Mrs. Wilson asked Doc, "What do you think of Hamp? He might be your son-in-law."

Doc said, "Well, he's got a good set of teeth."

---

[20] Ruth 1:16

W. Hamp Watson, Jr.

They bought the horse and it's been the best thing that ever happened in my life. An orphaned boy found another home and in Day Wilson I found, "This is the Day that the Lord hath made." Through her, in spite of her handicapping condition as a result of polio, have come three children that she "raised right," so that they have produced for us, so far, five of the most remarkable grandchildren in the world. I say this as a totally unbiased observer.

My uncle, Louis Matthews, had had a brief stint working at Wolfson's Dry Goods Store. He talked Mrs. Wolfson into putting up a horse on a raffle to bring in trade. He offered to keep the horse at my house until they gave it away. So at eleven years of age, I'd get on that horse and ride down Anthony street to ten-year-old Arthur Hardy's house. He'd come out and say, "Hamp, Hamp, let me ride your horse!"

I'd look down and say, "No, Arthur, you're too young to ride a horse."

The next Christmas, my horse had been long gone, given away on the raffle, and Arthur Hardy's Daddy had given him a horse of his very own. He came riding up Anthony Street, and I ran out in front of my house and said, "Arthur, Arthur, let me ride your horse!"

Arthur looked down at me and said, "No, Hamp, you're too old to ride a horse."[21]

Some time back on a trip to Warm Springs to get a new brace for Day, I had to wait while she saw the doctor. A young woman in her early twenties came wheeling up in her chair to the receptionist's desk. She was obviously a veteran of Warm Springs' experiences for the receptionist, Mrs. Grace Butts, immediately recognized her. She said, "Carla, how good to see you! What are you doing now?"

This opened up a torrent of joyous conversation in which Carla told of completing her college career and practice teaching in her wheel chair. She said, "And would you believe, I've got a teaching

[21] Galatians 6:7

W. Hamp Watson, Jr.

job in Florida starting this fall?" Nevertheless, afterward![22] Through it all!

When I was a child and went down to the chancel rail to take communion with my mother, I was fascinated by the fact that I couldn't get all the juice out of that little communion glass. So I turned my head up and stuck my tongue just as far up in there as it would reach to get that last little drop. When I did, I felt my mother's grip tighten on my arm so much that it was cutting off the circulation. And when we got home, she said, "Hampton, just what do you think you're doing when you take the Lord's Supper?"

That's not a bad question for a Christian to try to answer every time we partake of this brief, grave and still sacrament. Just what do we think we're doing?[23]

In the days when we were on the five-point Rochelle Circuit, I would preach at 10:00 at Pitts, 11:30 at Rochelle, and 12:30 at Kramer. One morning when Susan was a toddler, Day stayed home to get her ready and I was to pick them up as I swung by the parsonage in Rochelle on our way out to Kramer and lunch in a family home afterward. On Mother's Day, I completed church at Rochelle and started out to Kramer on my route past the parsonage.

Day had struggled to get herself and Susan dressed and they were waiting on the large front porch of the parsonage for me to pick them up. Day recounts it this way: "I saw Hamp turn the corner from the Fitzgerald Highway and head toward us. But as he approached the parsonage, he didn't even glance our way. I waved and waved as he passed. When he was completely out of sight and I had given up hope that he would stop or remember, I turned to Susan and said, 'Well, here we are—all dressed up and nowhere to go!'"

---

[22] Hebrews 12:11
[23] I Corinthians 11:29

W. Hamp Watson, Jr.

This was not the first or last time I had forgotten something really important, but what took the cake was the fact that I was preaching that day on 'The Christian Home.'[24]

At Colquitt, when Wade and Ann were about eight and six respectively, we acquired some sort of recording device. They were fascinated with it, and each wanted to say something or sing something into it. They began to wrestle over it. One particular time, Ann was successful in securing it as she snatched it from Wade. Before he could grab it again, she started singing into it, "*Let There Be Peace on Earth, and let it begin with me.*"[25]

Our daughter Ann reminded me of this story about her grandmother. Ma was in her bedroom sewing an outfit. She knew that a neighbor down the street was sick and that she should stop and go visit her. However, she wanted to finish the outfit, so she kept working. After a short time, the sewing machine jammed. She tried and tried to get the machine working again but could not. Finally, in exasperation, she decided to stop and go visit her neighbor. When she returned from her visit and sat back down to wrestle with the sewing machine, it worked with no problem.

Ma said, "I think somebody was trying to tell me something."

My son-in-law, Tim Bagwell, told me this:
"I pulled into the parking lot to let my wife, Susan, run into the store while I stayed outside listening to the radio in the car. Another car soon parked right in front of me. It caught my attention because driving the car was a nun dressed in her full nun's habit. Suddenly I realized that she was listening to the same radio station I was enjoying. How did I know? She was enthusiastically singing the song which was playing and to which I was listening:

---

[24] Ephesians 5
[25] Psalm 133:1

W. Hamp Watson, Jr.

"Torn between two lovers, feeling like a fool.
Loving both of you is breaking all the rules!"

It seemed odd and maybe a bit out of character.   I smiled.
The nun smiled, a bit chagrined. I nodded. She nodded. I think
we understood in that ever-so-brief moment that holiness does not
save us from the struggles of life. But God is with us."

Carlin McDonald who grew up in Baxley, Georgia, and
married my nephew, Charles W. Morris, is a golf-playing,
bridge-loving skiing enthusiast with an effervescent, bubbling
personality. In her spare time, she has managed to raise two super-
achieving children and to conceive and head up an annual "Shoe
the Children" event out in her home, Dallas, Texas. She, her
church, donors, and friends have put thousands of poor children
into shoes. These kids get to go to the stores of participating
merchants and pick out their shoes for themselves. This year, 2005,
was the nineteenth year of the shoe drive, and, as of this writing,
they had shoed 1,392 children with about twenty more to go.

But Carlin had never been called upon to play the role of
priest-pastor-comforter. Near the end of a college school term,
when she was expecting her two children home from college
momentarily, she was hosting a bridge club event in her home.
One of her bridge-playing companions had lost her son by suicide
just one month before. This was the first time that they were all
together again and an atmosphere of gloom hung heavy over the
room. They called on Carlin to lead them in the blessing for the
meal, feeling that she might be one who could include in that
prayer some comforting words about their friend's great loss.

Carlin doesn't remember the early words of her prayer or what
she tried to say to God on behalf of her bereaved friend, but about
the time she was finishing up, she was distracted, as her children
barrelled through the door coming home from college.

Carlin said, "I **do** remember how I closed the prayer. What I
said was, 'Bless these and all our many blessings. In Christ's name

W. Hamp Watson, Jr.

we pray.' Instead of saying, 'Amen," I said, 'Thank you and bye bye!!!!!!'"

As they all burst into laughter, the gloom lifted and receded a little from the room. As Carlin put it, "It turned out to be a good ice breaker in a tense situation!!!"

I told Carlin later, "Maybe it's a good thing that there was no golden-voiced, priest or pastor present to phrase a beautiful prayer with carefully chosen words and proper ascription. What you did did just fine!"

N ow you would expect a grandfather to tell this kind of story about his youngest granddaughter. On Halloween, Ann and three-year-old Sarah were out trick or treating. The lights at a house up a steep driveway were on, so they decided to stop there. They rang the bell and Sarah said to the lady answering the door, "Trick or treat!"

The lady looked down at Sarah and sadly said, "Oh honey, I don't have any candy."

Sarah immediately held out her bag of candy and said, "Here, you can have some of mine."

I f you think that sibling rivalry is not a reality with which the wise parent will have to deal, note this story by our daughter, Susan Bagwell.

"During the last few months of pregnancy, I began preparing our almost three-year-old son, John, for the upcoming addition to our family. We checked out books about being a big brother, bought a special T-shirt, and really discussed the change that was coming in our family with the arrival of a new baby. I thought we had done an excellent job until a conversation I had with John a few days before our second child, Emily, was born. John said, 'I understand that we are going to have a new baby. But who will be the baby's mother?'

I was a little surprised by this question but responded by telling John that I, of course, would be the baby's mother. With tears in his eyes and a quivering chin, John said to me, 'But you are **my** mother!'"

I need to tell this story to parents who somehow imagine that they will be able to filter out all of the information about sex and pro-creation from the televisions, radios, cell-phones, and computers of this generation. Our granddaughter Emily is grown now, but when she was eight, her mother shared with her the information that my son, Wade, and his wife, Betty, were expecting a second child. Their first was just two years of age at the time. Emily took in this information, then went back to her room to go to bed. Very shortly she came back out and said to her mother, "Was this a planned pregnancy?"

Shocked, Susan said, "Emily, why are you asking that question?"

Emily said, "Well Hamp is so young and I thought this might be having them too close together."

Susan then went into an explanation of how this spacing was just about the age difference between Emily and her older brother, John, and that had worked out very well. That seemed to satisfy her and she went on back to her room and went to sleep.

Who knows what she had heard, and when, and where?

M y mother came to Baxley, Georgia from her home in Talbot County, Georgia, leading singing for Bishop Warren A. Candler as he preached a revival at Baxley, when she was twenty years of age. She wound up marrying my father, who was a forty-year-old bachelor lawyer in Baxley. She sang a solo that week:

> *The Gospel Train is Comin'*
> *It's comin' round the bend...*
> *Get on board, little children!*
> *There's room for many a more!*

W. Hamp Watson, Jr.

That leads me to say that though it saddened me and broke my heart, as it always does when anyone breaks the fellowship, I really considered it sort of a compliment to our church at Wesley Monumental in Savannah when I got a letter from a member withdrawing membership. The letter said, "Your church is too all-inclusive." I don't know whether this was referring to the fact that all kinds of persons of all races, genders, and lifestyles were welcome to worship there. It could have been that. Or it could have been the fact that our Wesley Gardens facilities on Moon River had been recently shared by our youth with the racially mixed children of the homeless. Whatever the reason, we weren't going to change those tentative efforts to reach out to others, for we were a long way yet from being patterned and programmed like the kingdom.

That led me to think about Dr. William H. "Bill" Hinson's story about being in the Atlanta airport, rushing to catch his plane. As he tried to get on one of the underground shuttles, a fellow ahead of him attempted to get on, dragging his suitcase behind him. As he did, the suitcase got jammed in the shutting door, lights and bells and whistles went off, and the train came to a halt with the smell of burnt electrical wiring in the air.

Late already, Bill whirled and started running down the access corridor to catch his plane. As he did, he would come upon crowds of people waiting at the doors where that train was supposed to come pick them up. He began shouting out to them, "This train isn't coming!" They would just give him blank stares, as he rushed on.

Finally, in frustration, he reverted to South Georgian and began shouting, "This train ain't coming! This train ain't coming!" But still no one would make a move, as he kept running toward his plane.

I wonder how many people are waiting for the Gospel Train, thinking that only people like themselves will be on board, and they've never heard the message, "This train ain't coming!" It's like my mother sang, *"There's room for many a more!"*[26]

---

[26] Luke 13:22-30

W. Hamp Watson, Jr.

Index